# SUBSCRIBE TO THE BDB PODCAST

The #1 Podcast for businessmen to have success without sacrifice.

# THE

# MODERN

## DAY BUSINESS

# MAN

SUCCESS WITHOUT SACRIFICE

# THE

NICHOLAS BAYERLE

# MODERN
# DAY BUSINESS
# MAN

## SUCCESS WITHOUT SACRIFICE

LIFESTYLE
ENTREPRENEURS
PRESS
LAS VEGAS, NV

# TABLE OF CONTENTS

Subscribe to the BDB Podcast.................................................i

1.  Discover Your Purpose ....................................................1

2.  Pursuit of Greatness.......................................................13

3.  Become a Three-Dimensional Businessman ..........................27

4.  The 4 Stages of a Businessman's Life................................45

5.  YOU are your #1 Investment: Health .................................59

6.  The Power of Mentors ....................................................75

7.  The Power of Brotherhood..............................................89

8.  Traits of a Successful Businessman..................................101

9.  Why Businessmen Fail ...................................................119

10. Three Elements of a Successful Business............................131

11. Create a Power-Couple Relationship.................................139

12. Creating a Legacy..........................................................153

Join the Billion Dollar Brotherhood Facebook Group.................166

Grab exclusive trainings from me here
www.nicholasbayerle.com/ offers.........................................167

Attend the #1 Event for Businessmen .................................168

# DISCOVER YOUR PURPOSE

Our hearts raced together as we stepped out on stage in front of over 4500 people. It was like playing in the Super Bowl—the timer was counting down, and we were in the zone. We were not thinking about the actions we were taking or the words coming out of our mouths; all of that faded away as we locked into the moment. It all seemed like a blur until we got to the end of our keynote: "Your past can truly become your greatest platform." There was a second of silence as I saw 4500 sets of white eyeballs looking back at me. *Did I say the right words? Did they even care about what we had to say?* That second felt like a year until all 4500 people stood up and started cheering.

*"Your past can truly become your greatest platform."*

It had been a long journey to get to that stage—pains and struggles I thought would be a ceiling on my life forever, weighing me down for the rest of my life. As a man I experienced endless failures that happened when nobody was looking, when nobody was cheering—heck, when nobody was even thinking about me. But it's in those moments, the decisions you make when nobody is there, that your destiny is shaped.

Who knew that your greatest mess could also become your greatest message...

# What You Do Matters

On May 2, 2010, my life changed forever with a phone call: my friend of four years had committed suicide.

I was a terrible student, barely graduating high school. I just wanted to scrape by with the easiest classes because I really didn't see the purpose of being there at the time. So, I picked up guitar class. I had already started playing the year before, so I thought, *Who wouldn't want to play guitar and call it school?* So, that's what I did for three years.

In guitar class, we had a group of the same three people who sat next to each other. One of those three people was a girl named Jamie. For three years, we played guitar together. When I got to my senior year of high school, I decided not to do guitar again, so the only time we saw each other was in passing between fourth and fifth period. Every day, I remember passing Jamie, and each day, I gave her a head nod. I never really thought about how she felt, or how she was doing, until the day I received that heart-wrenching phone call. I didn't realize how much that moment awoke something inside of me until shortly before I decided to write this book.

Growing up, I was extremely self-conscious. I was self-conscious about the way I looked and what other people thought of me. I was 60 pounds overweight. If you break down the word "self-conscious," it means someone who is only aware of oneself. At this point in my life, I could only think about myself because of my lack of confidence.

In this book, you are going to learn and discover how I personally went from being this extremely self-conscious kid to the man I am today. I truly believe that confidence is the number-one attribute a successful businessman must master. Confidence is in the way you think, the way you present yourself, the way you talk, and the words you speak.

# You Are the Change

Have you ever looked off the side of a cliff before? Or maybe even the ledge of a tall building? I know many of you have even jumped off of large cliffs or rocks into water. If you have, then you know that feeling of hesitation at first, even though you know it will be okay—like jumping off the diving board into a pool for the first time. So, what is that feeling? It's that fear that keeps us alive. It's the fear that we may get hurt. It's something inside of us saying, "ARE YOU SURE YOU WANT TO DO THIS?"

Now imagine Jamie, searching in her heart for ANYTHING that would keep her from making that decision. What would it have taken for her to have not made that detrimental choice? A smile? A compliment? A friend? Someone who wasn't self-conscious like

I was? That's a question I don't know the answer to, but what I do know is that she is gone.

I remember after hearing the news, I cried like a baby, not fully comprehending what had just happened. I remember a few days later, the local church held a space for students, teachers, and family members to gather together in honor of Jamie. I watched as HUNDREDS of people turned up, just from word of mouth. My jaw dropped at the impact she had made in so many people, yet we were not able to impact her to that depth. I had never seen so many people gather together and not be able to change the situation. Or, at least we thought we couldn't. The one thing that we could do, and what I believe every man is called to do, is learn from every situation we encounter, good or bad.

So why am I opening up the book talking about suicide? Well, one of the reasons is for the story I'm about to tell you, and the other is because men have a four times higher percentage of suicide compared to women according to data from the Centers for Disease Control and Prevention. If you have ever felt this way before, I hope this book is a tool to gain a greater purpose and inspires you to rise up as a leading businessman. The world is looking and waiting for men to rise up, to live in their destinies, and to change lives for the better. You are that man the world is looking for.

About six months after Jamie's passing, I remember driving home in my truck around 12:30 a.m., crying my eyes out, wishing that God would use me as his vessel. I wanted to be someone who could speak those words that could transform lives and impact someone to choose life over death.

I wanted to be someone that could save a person from making the same choice that Jamie made. So, as I drove, I decided in that moment that I didn't care if God or anyone else showed up. I was going to show up. Logically, I thought, *Well, if there are only a handful of people showing up, wanting to be used, and making a big difference in the world, maybe I will get some direction from God.*

Sitting in my red, 1997 Nissan Hardbody stick-shift truck with a white camper shell, I made the decision to listen and take action. A few minutes later, I felt a tug telling me to get off on an exit where nobody lived, still 15 minutes from my house. I remember thinking that it was stupid, but I had just told myself that I was ready to live this life with purpose. When I got off the exit, I turned left and looked around, but there was nobody in sight. Finally, I saw someone walking on the street. As I got closer, I started to see that he was not wearing any shoes. I got even closer and saw that he was tattooed from head to toe. So, at 18 years old, I thought, *PERFECT*, not worrying about anything bad happening to me. I had a feeling in my gut telling me that I should stop for him, so I made a U-turn and waited at the street corner. Smart, right?

I watched him come around the corner, and right as he did, he RUSHED my truck at full speed. In that moment, I had no clue what to do or say. I felt my heart racing because at that moment I thought he could have had a gun on him. Right before he got to my truck, I just blurted out something, and the craziest thing happened. If you want to know what happened next, which is one of the craziest events I've ever experienced, you will have to keep reading till the end. That night radically shifted me and why I do what I do today.

# You are Called

Have you ever had an epiphany, or had words come into your mind that really resonated with you? When I was 18 years old, I heard this quote from God that forever shaped my decision-making process. I heard it when I decided to leave college and pursue my dreams. I knew that people would be disappointed in me and think of me as a failure: *"I would rather do what I know is right and fail, than do what I already know is wrong and succeed."*

### *"I would rather do what I know is right and fail, than do what I already know is wrong and succeed."*

For me, this meant that I would rather do what I knew was right, even if I failed in front of everyone else, than succeed in everyone else's eyes, knowing that I did the wrong thing. Success becomes something completely different when you experience this. Many people are called, but few are chosen in this world.

You are reading this book right now because you are a man who has been chosen. Chosen people are led. They have dreams, visions, aspirations, and goals inside of them. All they have to do is take one step at a time, one exit at a time, one left turn at a time, one U-turn at a time, one stop on the street corner at a time, which eventually leads to a huge impact. Your gut, your intuition, and the voice of God are the three things that trump EVERYTHING else in the world. I can't tell you how many times a week someone in the Billion Dollar Brotherhood Facebook Group or Instagram says to me, "I'm trying to find my purpose" or "I want to do all of these things; I'm just not sure what to do." That quote makes making a choice easy.

When I heard that quote, I was on my mother's living room floor in 2011. I wanted to go to multiple countries and serve the poor, but the trip alone was over $4,000, which, for an 18 year old, was quite a bit. Especially one who had never had a job before. I remember sitting on my floor, problem-solving all the ways I could get $4,000, and one of the quickest ways I thought of would be to go ask people for money. In that moment though, I felt like I wasn't supposed to do that; that I wasn't even supposed to bow my head and freaking pray for it because it was going to happen by faith. When you are walking in power and your destiny, it doesn't even matter. Opportunities will come. So, without sending out mass support letters, I sat in my house with my stomach turning, looking at my PayPal account every day. I felt sick every day about the thought of making this happen. Then, all of the sudden, on the last day when I needed a deposit to hold my spot for the trip, my Navy Seal now-mentor deposited $750 into my bank account. I ended up going on that trip, which was fully paid for without my contributing. I got invited to another trip that was going to be $2,800 extra, just for flights, which I did not have. The people putting on the mission trips asked me if I had the money, and I said, "Of course, I do." I had a tiny bit of cash for the first flight on my debit card, but because I was so broke, I called my mom and asked her to swipe $2,800 on her credit card. I told her that I would pay her back when I got back home.

I ended up going to Bulgaria, Turkey, Greece, France, Scotland, London, South Africa, and Mozambique. I did have one problem though: I forgot to book my flight home. After staying up all night, the cheapest flight home I could find was $1,200, which I had to have someone else buy again because of my debit card issues. By the time I got home, and after paying back the $1,200, I had $584 left in my bank account and owed my mom $2,800. I knew at the time that the math didn't line up, and again, I had no physical clue how I was going to pay her back. So, one day, I was at church and I looked at the money in my bank account. I didn't yet know how to produce money, but I did know one principle of life, which is that if you give, you will be given back to. A spiritual law I learned and fully practice every day. I believe that more blessed is the hand that gives rather than receives. So, I decided in that moment to do the exact opposite of what most people would. I gave all my money away. In the blink of an eye, I had no money and owed my mother $2,800.00. If I didn't pay her, it would not be good since she didn't tell my step dad.

Two weeks later, I walked into my mom's townhome with a fat stack of cash that I left on the counter for her. $2,800.00. When I came back from the trips, a few families heard the stories of what happened and felt like sowing into me doing more trips. I felt like a baller, and I learned something extremely valuable from this crazy process of living 100 percent by faith. I could have gone out there and worked for the money, begged for the money, stole for the money, and the list goes on. Deep down inside I knew that I would have rather done what I felt was right and failed in front of everyone and not gone on the trips, than do the wrong thing and somehow go on that trip. To be truly successful, you are going to want to live your life the same way, and when you do, it creates a space for miracles to happen.

# You Are Three Dimensional

This book isn't meant for the average person who wants to be average. It was written for the man who wants to live to his maximum potential. It doesn't matter where the man is; what does matter that he is in a place to see exponential growth. Going and growing through this book, you will learn the skill sets to have it all; to become a **Three-Dimensional Businessman** prospering in **health**, **wealth**, and **relationships** in a way that the world has never seen before.

The majority of men live very one dimensionally, only prospering in one area of our life, which keeps us stuck, unfulfilled, and doesn't serve those around us, literally taking away everything we are working for as we build it. It's like working on a house every day that someone then rips to the ground every night, only to start over again. The reason why you will see this transformation is because you and I are different. I always say that *"information + application = transformation."*

While some look at a book and wonder if it's worth reading, others read it and never apply the information. Then there are people like us. When we see something valuable, we not only take it in; we think about it, chew on it, write it out, and apply it. We allow it to shift our daily actions until it actually changes our results. Pat yourself on the back if you made it this far. This means you are that type of person that takes the strategies and principles in this book and applies them.

One of my biggest pet peeves with books, and why I don't read a lot, is they are only relevant for a time. They teach tactics rather than strategy. Tactics only work for a certain period of time because tactics are always changing. What works on social media right now won't be relevant in a few years from now. The concepts in this book will stand the test of time. They are truths that are not just for today, or the year that this book was written, but are foundational truths that men will live by thousands of years from now. This book is not for a specific industry that may come or go—this is for the businessman who wants to build and succeed in every area and to have success without sacrifice.

While most of the world from day one focuses on success and transformation from the outside in, we do it differently at Billion Dollar Body. There are many people in the world that people like from a distance. It's not that hard to put up a front and a facade to have people love you from a distance. Many successful people have done this in the past; they had everyone who they didn't know loving them while the people closest to them didn't. This is not true success.

True success starts first with the impact on yourself and those closest to you, then outward. Nobody should trust a man whose family life is broken, who is dishonest, and who treats people badly.

Here's a saying that I live by: *"Some things are better caught than taught."*

What does this mean? Well, Jim Kwik, brain and learning expert, said that "kids learn best from their environment and watching other people." This still applies to adults and probably the reason why the quote "You are the average of the five people you hang around" is so popular.

### *"Some things are better caught than taught."*

I remember golfing (and being horrible at it) with my good friend who was also a professional golfer. Being around him transformed my swing and ability to play the game. But one thing that nobody would have ever guessed was that because he dipped chewing tobacco every day and spit while he golfed, I spit too, even though I never used chewing tobacco. I picked up not just the things I wanted, but other things as well. The power is receiving from the environment, which shows that it matters who you are around and learning from, because some things are better caught than taught.

Has your life ever changed in an instant? It could be getting accepted into a new school, moving, divorce, realizing that you have a health condition, etc. Change can happen in instant. Sometimes it takes a long time to get to the tipping point though. I'm sure you have had times in your life where things changed for the negative in an instant; if that can happen, so can the positive.

I first learned this when things took a turn for the worse. Since then, I have learned from these different times and have shifted my perspective around it, but perception is reality. At 13 years old, I told my father I wanted to be the best motocross racer in the world. He looked at me and told me I would never be the best. This crushed me and sent me into a spiral that caused me to gain 60 pounds, go through high school with less than a 2.0 GPA, and transformed every area of my life. I will share more of this story later in the book.

Years later, at 17 years old, it changed again. A kid came to my school with fruit. It seems simple and stupid, yet when the time is right, the shift happens, I asked him, "What the heck are you doing with fruit?" He then told me that his boxing coach had put him on a meal plan to get him to weigh in at the correct weight and perform at his best. So, I went home and asked my mom to buy me fruits. This made an everlasting shift. I lost 60 pounds in six months without going to the gym once, all because of a moment.

All of the sudden, the shift happened:

1. There was a plan that I could follow and be successful in.
2. How I fueled and treated myself affected my performance.

This book is that moment for you; huge or enormous, this is that moment. So before flipping to the next chapter, now is the time to accept that no matter what, you are going to hit your goal and live the life of a Three-Dimensional Businessman. We hear stories from different times throughout history of great victories that were won because defeat was not an answer. This is your moment to go all in and do life at a whole new level.

# Chapter 1 Action Items:

Evaluate and assess where you are at right now with the principles mentioned in this chapter.

1. What are you self-conscious about right now that is holding you back? What can you do today to overcome it?

   _____

   _____

2. How is your environment negatively or positively impacting your life? Write down the things you can improve on.

   _____

   _____

3. Are you demonstrating the law of giving? How can you practice it more?

   _____

   _____

4. Are you stepping out in faith towards your goals and dreams? If not, why are you afraid of failing?

   _____

   _____

2

# PURSUIT OF GREATNESS

Inside of every man is greatness, along with a longing for that greatness to shine. Some people try to hide it because of past experiences, the fear of success, the fear of failure, and what people might think. But every single one of us wants to do something great, reach our full potential, and be recognized for what we do. They say recognition is so powerful that babies cry for it and men die for it.

Much like you, I have always wanted to be the best at everything I do. Heck, I would say I'm delusional. I genuinely believe that I could be the best basketball player in the world, even though I suck and am 5'7". I don't know if this is something that is in our DNA or the way that we grew up, or a little bit of both. I remember my earliest lesson about greatness was given to me by my dad at two years old. I got my first bicycle, and for most people, this is the time to get training wheels because that's what you do when you get a bike, right? You need something to keep you upright; something that keeps you from falling over.

Here is the first mistake with that. Nobody on this planet has ever gotten stronger from a crutch. Crutches can be great if you are BROKEN and you need to heal, but even then, they don't make you stronger. They keep you from getting hurt. People who start wearing glasses don't get better sight; they have a crutch, and their eyes keep getting worse. People that start using walkers don't get better from using walkers; they have a new crutch that they can't live without.

See, most people use training wheels to keep themselves from falling, but at the same time, it keeps them from learning how to balance. So, what did my dad do? He said, "Son, I'm not going to put training wheels on your bike." So, did I fall more than the average person? Sure, probably. But ultimately, I learned a good lesson: Unless something is going to strengthen you for the future, don't use it. Training wheels slow down the process of learning and are not used in the future, so ditch them. My dad's actions made me the youngest kid in the world at the time to start racing bicycles. Greatness comes from eliminating crutches.

### *"If you're not first, you're last."*

The next stage in my life was motocross. Since it was my dad's dream to ride, he then groomed me to do what he wanted to do. I started racing motocross at the age of four, and the buildup of wanting to be the best started rising within me. I truly believed in the saying: *"If you're not first, you're last."* I totally agreed with the statement. I didn't know why everyone was laughing and making jokes about it. Second place was the first loser. *Doesn't everyone think this way?* I wondered when people told me to take it easy with how competitive I was. Little did I know that winning was a skill and a personality trait that every successful businessman embodies.

# You Are a Money Magnet

I am not a morning person, so when people ask me my about my 10-step morning routine, they won't be impressed. My routine is pretty simple. Every day I wake up, drink 20oz of water, eat breakfast, and spend at least 30 minutes sipping my coffee just thinking or talking with my wife. I then journal my to-dos for the day and get to work. I made a coffee mug that says, "I'm a Money Magnet." It's not a materialistic thing, I just want to be reminded that I am a money magnet. Zig Ziglar said it best: "Money is not everything, but it ranks right up there with oxygen." You will experience more opportunities to grow and to give back if you have more money. It's a reality that applies to us all. When I didn't have money to provide for myself, I wasn't able to help thousands of kids like we do know by partnering with nonprofit The Winning Edge. When I didn't have money, I couldn't take my girlfriend, my now wife, on a date for her birthday. I literally went to Trader Joes and picked up a few of her favorite things because that's all I could afford at the time. Having money has given me opportunities to invest in my network, in myself, provide for my wife, and give back to the causes and people I believe in.

> **"Money is not everything, but it ranks right up there with oxygen."**

Wherever you are currently in your money situation, know that you have the power to change it because building wealth is an obligation for every man. Every man deep down inside knows it. They can feel it; they can taste it. We as men are hormonally wired by dopamine, and when we make money, we get a dopamine high. As a modern-day businessman who wants to have success without sacrifice, you must master the art of money.

# There are three core components to making money:

1.  The act of production, or the ability to go create money through the exchange of value.
2.  The act of keeping money and knowing how to steward it well.
3.  The act of investing and taking the money that you have been given and growing it.

# Production

The very first of these three is production, the making of money. My father once told me something that would change my outlook on this forever. Growing up, my father ran and worked in the carpet-cleaning and flood-restoration business, along with my uncle who then went into many other businesses. I don't know what it would have been like if my dad had a regular 9-to-5 job. I just saw my dad work hard every day inside of his business, "Cleanday Carpet Care." My mom and dad split up when I was four, so from that side, I got to see my mom work hard as well, which felt very similar. So, it wasn't the work, or what they were working on, that transformed me; it was this mindset shift that seeded something inside of me from then until now. My dad looked at me one day and he said, "You know what I would do if I lost everything?" I thought his answer would be, "Go to work for someone else like Mom did." He said, "If worse came to worst, all I would have to do is grab a lawn mower and weed whacker and be able to provide for myself."

The lesson I learned was that money always follows value. Value, by definition, is solving more problems for more people. Warren Buffett said, "Price is what you pay. Value is what you get." People have problems and needs that have to be solved, and when you solve them or fulfill them, you get paid. He taught me that if I just had simple skills, the worst-case scenario is that I would still be fine. So, around 12 years old, I went out there and gave it a shot. I went out and started Nick's Lawn Care. The slogan was: "We mow it and blow it." Yes, I meant for it to be sexual. I was a middle schooler. We went out there on our bikes, printed out flyers using clipart, and started to knock on doors and schedule appointments with our pens and paper.

We looked for the most jacked-up yards that were overgrown and knocked on their doors. We gave them a quote, did the job, and then set them up on a retainer of maintenance work.

A few months later, I had two guys working for me, and a couple thousand dollars saved up in my drawer. I had learned the principle that money follows value, and value is simply solving more problems for more people. I also learned that even when things get worse, it's still fine because if you can get good at sales, you will always be able to produce. Over the years, I've learned how to sell on the phone, on stage, and even through Facebook Messenger. I tell my clients to study how I speak, my body language, and the words I use because everything is for a purpose. How did I learn to sell hundreds of thousands of dollars' worth of product? It was through my mentor, Cole Hatter, and all the network marketing experience I acquired in the past. We will talk about the power of mentors later on in this book.

# Keeping Money

Most people think that if they just had money, they would be fine. They dream of having that big break in business, they complain about how Donald Trump had it easy with his million-dollar loan, and they fantasize over winning the lottery. Even the man who has mastered production is incomplete without being able to keep his money. I too used to dream of winning the lottery. I remember the excitement of my family playing every weekend. It even got to the point where I decided to look up what other families did when they won the lottery. Deep into my research I discovered something that changed my life forever. The majority of people who win the lottery actually end up going broke again and actually wish they would have never won in the first place.

When you get results that you always wanted, yet don't know how to actually manage your finances, you end up sabotaging yourself right back to where you were at in the first place. It's like giving someone the body of their dreams without any clue of how to maintain it, just to watch themselves get fat and out of shape all over again.

Through coaching many successful businessmen, I have seen a lot of kids who are just like I was go from making a few thousand dollars a month to hundreds of thousands of dollars a month, yet their lifestyles would climb just as rapidly as their incomes. Ryan Blair, one of the first people I looked up to in business, told me about how in his early twenties he had built a company and sold it which yielded him one million dollars. Not a bad pay day for a young kid, right? Because of that influx in cash he felt like a baller and started trying to keep up with other ballers. Within the year he was completely broke; he had learned how to produce yet never learned how to keep. My Navy Seal mentor was heavily against this type of behavior and gave me a number to shoot for that I still follow today. "Live off 50% of your income." He taught me that if I only made $3000.00 a month, I should live off $1500. You are probably thinking the same thing I was: *How the hell am I supposed to live off that?* Well, he told me, "If you don't like it, then change how much you make, just don't change how much you live off of." So, from that day forward I decided to make it a goal to get as close as I could to living off 50% and make that the new normal in my life. "If everyone did that, then everyone would be fine," he said." There are many people that can produce quick money, and then it's quickly gone. If you want to embark on a journey of a life that has it all, it's time to apply the concept of keeping money in a storehouse to make sure the kingdom is full for any season.

### *"Live off 50% of your income."*

# Growing Money

The last area of money is growing money, the phase that has caused some of the financial titans to increase their wealth exponentially and compound it over the years. All of the top financial advisors in the world agree that there are a few investments that you can make that superseded all the rest. When I first got into business, I tried to skip straight to the investing side of money by investing in real estate and the stock market like most people would. Yet as I studied the 1% of the 1% who were the wealthiest in the world, I realized something different about them. Many of them had made money and lost it many times yet were confident to build it back again. And with my father and uncle's business' taking a massive hit in 2008, I knew that I had to figure out this billionaires' mindset. The billionaires' mindset is that if you take a poor person and make him head over a kingdom of wealth, he will turn it into rubble again. Yet if you take a king and place him in the poorest conditions, he will rise up again. Warren Buffett sums it up like this: "There is one investment that supersedes all the rest, and that's the investment in yourself." Beyond that the second most lucrative place a businessman can invest his money is back into his own business, the place where he is producing to expand his capacity.

There was a story about a few men that had been given money. Each one of them were given a certain amount, and the lender was going to come back after a certain amount of time to see what they had done with the money and the profits they were able to create. One of the men had doubled his money, the second had seen 50% growth, and the other man decided to do something different. This man decided to dig a hole and place his money underground for the fear of losing all of the money the man had given him. Thinking that the lender would be pleased, he dug up the money to show him how well he did with his money. The lender looked at him displeased and said, "Couldn't you have at least placed it into a bank so it would at least gain interest?" Then he took that man's money and gave it to the man who had doubled his money. He then took the men who had grown money and made them rulers of towns based on the growth of the money.

To be a Three-Dimensional Businessman we are called to be the man in the story that doubled his portion, not just the one who digs a hole to not lose it all. Learn the three stages of money, master them, and you will be given more than riches. The best way to do all three steps is to surround yourself with mentors and people who are already doing it. Focus on the people who are actually living the life you want and not the ones who have two cents about the subjects because they are only worth two cents. (None of the advice I put in these chapters is financial advice, and one should consult a professional before following any of it.)

# You Have a Purpose

Even though I was producing money at 12, I was still lacking a very important thing as a man. A thing that without it, causes men to die.

Not just internally and mentally, but actually causes them to pass away. During the Holocaust, someone did a study on the families of concentration camp members because the conditions in the camps were so extreme and brutal. These people were living on very little, if any—no food or water—yet somehow, they survived just from the simple thought of reconnecting and seeing their families or significant others again. They noticed that when someone got news of the passing of the person that they were holding onto, they passed away in three days like clockwork. Their vision of what life would be like when they got out of the camp was now gone. Without VISION, men perish. Vision will keep you alive even without food or water and in the worst living conditions.

Proverbs 29:18 *"Where there is no vision, the people perish."*

All I had for a vision was to be the best motocross racer in the world. I had no reason to cut lawns. I had no reason to save up a bunch of money. So, I took my profits, shut down that business, and went back to focusing on being the best motocross racer in the world. The problem is, as a man, the pressures of becoming the best, the pressures of wanting to fulfill the standard that we think the world and our fathers have for us, is a weight that is tough to bear.

I remember consistently getting anxiety before I would go ride motocross. I had so much fear built up around it—fear that I wasn't good enough, that I wouldn't perform enough. Faith and fear have similar definitions. With both fear and faith, you are believing something that you cannot see will happen. I was crippled and strangled by fear. It got to the point where I would gag myself before going and riding because I was so nervous that I wanted any excuse to skip it. Even to the point of scratching the back of my throat to throw up a little blood for good effect. This taught me something really powerful as well, even though I hated every minute of it. My dad never cared that I was throwing up; we were going anyway. I remember there was never a day that I would go to the track and ride that I wasn't happy. Pretty much every time I decided to go, I was glad I did, yet fear crippled me. The buildup of pressure, family issues, anxiety, and everything else started to cripple me to the point that I was just looking for a way out. I had gotten to the point that I needed someone to believe in me, when all the sudden, the biggest blessing in disguise happened.

### *"Where there is no vision, the people perish."*

One day, when I was in my bedroom, I heard my dad walking down the hallway through the kitchen and into the garage where he would commonly go hang out and drink beer. I came out of my room, followed him through the kitchen, and when I was headed down the stairs into the garage, I finally told my dad. "DAD, I want to be the best motocross racer in the world. I want to quit school, get a tutor, and get on the road so we can be the best."

I thought this was the moment he had been waiting for. *This will do it for sure, and finally all my problems will go away. My father will notice me, believe in me, and we will go make it happen together.* Maybe my memory is skewed as a kid, but I only remember my dad telling me he loved me was when he was drinking. As a little boy, his approval was the only thing that mattered to me.

Then the blessing in disguise happened. He looked at me and said without even thinking, "You will never be the best." Deep down inside, I think I was hoping this would be said; the very thing that deep down I already believed and just needed someone else to confirm, and it happened.

This was the first time that my life was transformed in a moment. A single second shifted my perspective. What was the transformation? More anxiety and depression. I quit motocross, started playing video games, and just wanted to get as far as I could from anyone that could hurt me or even believe in me. Over the next couple of years, I very rarely spoke to my father. I locked myself in my room at my mom's house, playing upward of 60 hours of World of Warcraft straight with no sleep. The video games gave me a purpose again, and the dopamine high was addictive. I had given up on everything. I gave up on the only vision I had in life, gave up on myself, and my health. My self-esteem had plummeted, and my self-consciousness rose, as I had more issues and things people could make fun of me for. I gained 60 pounds of pure fat, I dropped my grades in school to below a 2.0, and throughout all of high school, I never had one girlfriend. I had hit rock bottom. My vision had perished, and I was a dead kid with a beating heart.

I did so terrible in school that I had to go to summer school every year. It ended up coming down to my senior year where literally nobody thought I was going to graduate. I didn't even get a graduation card because it came as a shock even to me that I had actually passed! Just like that, the moment shifted my life for the negative in an instant.

If that is possible, so is the shift for the positive in an instant. Reading this book will be your moment. I remember coming to school one day, wearing the same damn sweatshirt I had worn every single day for the last year. Around the hood, the sun had taken away all of its color. As I sat there, sweating my ass off in 110-degree heat, acting like everything was okay, a kid decided to pull out a bag of fruit from his backpack. When he pulled out the bag, I was confused. *What the heck is he doing?* I was on the cinnamon roll and chocolate milk diet. In the winter, I would drink hot chocolate, and in the summer, I would drink chocolate milk. Yet this guy was doing it differently, so I asked him, "Why the heck are you eating fruit?"

That is when the next blessing happened. He told me that he was a boxer, and his trainer had put him on a meal plan to help him weigh in at the correct weight and perform his best.

All of a sudden, it clicked for me. My situation could be changed by a plan, and not only that, it would make me perform better. I realized there are two types of men out there who don't take action:

Someone who is extremely motivated yet lacks the clarity and plan to take action.

Someone who knows the exact plan to take yet has no motivation.

I was the first one. As soon as I saw that there was a plan, I took action, and boom—just like that, I dropped 60 pounds in six months, which caused me to reconnect with my father. The first pillar of every man's life that can never be outsourced is his health. It's something nobody else can do for you and that directly impacts every area of your life. The value others have for you will never exceed the value you have for yourself. You show that value through how you take care of yourself.

A few months after I had dropped the weight, I realized that I had transformed my physical body, yet there was still something missing. I didn't have the whole package. Greatness can never be achieved with a lack of prosperity in all areas of life: mental, physical, spiritual, and emotional. So, even after achieving a six pack, I still was lost and didn't know exactly what to do.

I realized that I needed a vision for every area of my life. Not just my health but also my relationships and career. If we men lack this powerful God-given vision, we will fall short of our true potentials.

*"Greatness can never be achieved with a lack of prosperity in all areas of life: mental, physical, spiritual, and emotional."*

# Chapter 2 Action Items:

Evaluate and assess where you are at right now with the principles mentioned in this chapter.

1. What was your childhood dream? Did you feel like you were born to do something great?

   _____

   _____

2. What are the things you can work on to make more money?

   _____

   _____

3. What are the things you can work on to keep money?

   _____

   _____

4. What are the things you can work on to grow money?

   _____

   _____

5. What's your current vision for your health, wealth and relationships?

_____

_____

3

# BECOME A THREE-DIMENSIONAL BUSINESSMAN

My first business focused on health because that's where my first transformation took place. I thought deep down that if we could fix men's health, everything else would fall into place. After 600 one-on-one sessions, I found out that wasn't the case. It was like I was patching up a very large hole on a boat, but there were other areas still letting water in. As I was coaching these men, we would spend 25% of our time focusing on just their health, then the other times talking about their relationships and businesses. It felt super awkward at first because I wasn't paid to talk with them about or help them with these other areas of life. The discovery was that each area affected each other, and if we were not equipped and given an example of a life that has it all, we will constantly go through life trying to pick up the pieces. Have you ever seen someone picking things up off the floor, but their hands are getting so full that the more they are picking up, the more they are dropping? Even though I don't believe in "balance," where you can perfectly do everything you want every single day. I do believe there is a way to build in habits and thought patterns that keep you from sacrificing the important things in your life.

*"I do believe there is a way to build in habits and thought patterns that keep you from sacrificing the important things in your life."*

When you go to the doctor due to pain on the right side of your back, there is a good chance it actually isn't your right side that's causing it. That's just where the symptom is flaring up. It's usually from a different part of the body out of alignment. If we focus on just the symptoms and don't go for the root of the problem, then the "weed" grows back. When a man came our way and he was struggling with his health, it was hardly ever just health that was the problem. It may have been the pressure and problems with his systems and schedules in his business. Or maybe he was having relationship issues at the time, and when something had to give, it ended up being his health. So instead of solving the root cause, people go after symptoms and chase them around their entire lives only to NEVER get ahead. The Three-Dimensional Businessman cures this root problem forever.

How you do one thing is how you do everything. To be the most trusted husband, business partner, family member, friend, CEO, etc., you have to build that trust. The three areas in life that we explained above are all three areas that cannot be outsourced; the bottleneck stops with you. Sure, someone can deliver flowers, someone can go shopping for you, and someone can do sales. But ultimately, you are the leader of your business. You are the person moving and eating the food; you are the man leading as a king in your relationship. Nobody wants to outsource the intimate stuff. To build massive trust and momentum, it takes first accepting the reality of responsibilities that every man has, and the areas of those that are his core duties. These are those areas, and the only way to build trust with yourself and others is to make them a priority; know that how you do one thing is how you do everything.

There are really three core responsibilities that are core areas for every man: health, wealth, and relationships. Everything that matters in a man's life falls into those categories. Most men are living one- or two-dimensional lives, prospering at one or two at a time, while always rotating through failure in one of the three core areas. For me, I was personally failing in every single one of the areas all at once; I guess you could have called me a zero-dimensional businessman.

Success will first start in the mind before it makes its way into reality. Being 60lbs overweight, single, and broke was not the issue. My issue was between my two ears. The self-sabotage, consistently doing things that I didn't want to do. Living in regret, not knowing or having the power to change my situation, or even the REASON to change my situation.

I was so ashamed of who I was that I would lock myself up, playing video games every chance I could get, completely ignoring the outside world and every opportunity that came my way.

Then I become a Two-Dimensional Businessman. At 20 years old, I practically had it all. I had my health. I was in the best shape of my life, and had my beautiful wife, who I had just married. However, I was missing one dimension that quickly smacked me in the face: WEALTH. Most people don't have this struggle; it's usually a different combination. This combo of prospering in my health and relationship but struggling with wealth led me to a very interesting place. A place where I started doing something that I didn't love, just to get by. Something that caused me to be away from my wife the majority of the day. Something that caused me to have to "GEL OUT" at the end of the day. All of a sudden, the necessity of finding balance in the wealth category ended up taking a massive toll on my health and my relationship. This is the constant cycle that every businessman in the world goes through, a constant juggle, constant roller coasters. It's kind of like the natural disasters back in the day. With no real sign, they would happen. Nowadays, we have technology that can inform us of what's going on so that we can move and evacuate when needed.

The MISSION of the Modern Day Businessman is to create SUCCESS (which every man reading this wants, and this will give it to you at a higher level than ever before) WITHOUT SACRIFICE. We want to literally change the dictionary definition of "businessman" to something that you cannot achieve with sacrifice in your personal life or home. That this book and movement will be a turning point for MEN that is almost as profound as BC and AD. That this movement will so dramatically shift the direction of men's lives that world leaders, countries, and top organizations will be flocking to ask how to set their foundation up for success; to have the FRUIT and results of what I'm going to share with you. YOU, as the man, will be the testament. Not a book, not a teaching, not a video, but a movement leading by example.

# BDB Power Statement:

I have a vision

I walk in power and confidence

I'm equipped for every challenge

I surround myself with the best to become my best

I value my body, my word, and my relationships

I am a Three-Dimensional Businessman

# How to achieve it all

So how do you have success in all areas? That's a question I've dug into for the last seven years of building different businesses. The first way is through your environment and the accountability that comes along with it. It is one of the strongest forces out there. We do this through The Billion Dollar Brotherhood, which is a community of other powerful men that have similar values. I will talk the power of Brotherhood in a later chapter, but I'm a firm believer that your environment and what people value around you what you will value. When I was making $2,000 a month, I surrounded myself with people who were making $10,000 a month. When I was first trying to get fit, I had a roommate who was shredded. Now I surround myself with a select few who have big businesses, great marriages, and value their physical and spiritual health. I don't hang around people who like to party every weekend, sleep around, and live undisciplined lives.

## *"I haven't seen anything positive come out of men hiding and isolating themselves."*

Since running a men's company, I've seen the difference between marketing for men and the things they struggle with compared to women. One of main differences is men go into a "cave." Dr. John Gray, author of the famous book *Men Are from Mars Women Are From Venus*, talks about how men retreat to a cave when emotional things happen whereas most women talk with people when emotional things happen. I haven't seen anything positive come out of men hiding and isolating themselves. Maybe you have been there before, scrolling social media without ever commenting, liking, or messaging anyone, not responding to texts or phone calls, giving excuses so you can be alone. I've been there before. My wife used to go to all the networking events, and I would stay home. I honestly can't believe I used to be that guy. Showing up to events, coaching calls, and attending social gatherings isn't easy when you are going through challenges. However, those are the things that got me the solutions to overcome the challenge. Those were the greatest breakthroughs because as men, we need to get better at asking for help and not wallowing in depression or hopelessness. The reason most men fail is because of seclusion. I want to dive deep into the psychology of it and how our society of "social media relationships" rather than real relationships is giving us a false sense of community. There are two main reasons why men go into seclusion.

The first reason is they believe that they have to be prospering and doing well in life to have community. Meaning that once everything is GREAT, then they will decide to connect with people and ask for help. This is the guy that needs to go put his head down and figure everything out on his own. The man that disappears at the first sign of struggle. So, he goes into a loop where every time he is prospering (which is a very small window because he has only found purpose in struggle), he decides to surround himself with people and community. Then, guess what? A problem occurs, and he decides that there is a correlation; it's been the lack of focus and problem solving alone that has created this, so he leaves the very community that can support and uplift him and goes back to doing everything on his own. He musters up just enough willpower to get back to stability and burn out, where he finally feels like he can surround himself with others and until he decides to go hide again with his problems.

I have been this man before and seen so many men struggle all by themselves. That is why The Billion Dollar Brotherhood is growing every single day; men are realizing that a trustworthy, supportive community is powerful. That is why our event, BDB Live, sells out every single year. Men are finally coming together and realizing the power of brotherhood. Being the facilitator brings me purpose.

The second reason a man goes into seclusion is that they feel they can only ask for help if they are failing. This is the man that decides to only jump into community when he needs a quick fix. He is on his deathbed in an area of his life, then he frantically reaches out to anything, he buys anything, he does anything to get out of his hole to have stability. Then, when he gets out of survival and into stability, he disappears. He believes that help is only needed and community is only needed when there is a major problem. He believes that when he is successful, what is the point? Otherwise known as not continually doing what made you successful in the first place. The community is what helped him succeed, and when he is in momentum, he decides to leave. I remember this funny fact hitting me when I looked at myself. I had first gotten into business, and one of the first things I did was make a list of potential prospects, reached out, and followed up over and over again throughout the month. I remember working REALLY, REALLY hard one month and nothing happened. So, what did I do? I decided I wasn't going to work harder the next month because it just wasn't worth the squeeze. All of a sudden, deals started closing easier than ever. So, what did I say, not knowing about this concept? "WHY THE HECK WAS I WORKING SO HARD?!" I didn't realize that I was riding the momentum of all the hard work I had put in the month before. I worked hard, then stopped. I reaped the harvest from the hard work the next month while I wasn't working hard. Then, all a sudden, not working hard would cause me to fail the next month, which would get me to work hard, which didn't produce a result, so I would let off the gas and start seeing results again. Sounds crazy, right? It happens all of the time to business owners.

Just as this is a cycle, seclusion is a cycle that keeps us from growing. Because of this cycle, we look for ANY type of comfort in the world we can get our hands on. Sex, drugs, alcohol, video games, working out (yeah, I said it), work (yeah, I said it), food—anything to get our fix and our mind of the real problems we have.

My first run-in with addiction was when I was 14 years old, and this went on until I was 17. I remember seeing a friend of mine play a video game that looked so epic that I wanted to get it. So, I put it on my Christmas list that year. I remember getting all of these things for Christmas but never saw the game come out. I was so happy with what I had that I really didn't even remember the game at the time. Then, at the very end of the night, I was handed a more powerful drug for a 14-year-old, high-achieving "be the best" personality than cocaine and oxycodone combined: a video game. Without my family knowing, this became my lifeline and the very thing that made up every decision I made—where I would go, what I would commit to. This addiction drove my entire life like an addict who can't leave his house. When I was away from it, it was like a detox, a constant thought, always wanting to leave everything early to get back to the thing that gave me comfort, purpose, and ultimately, false fulfillment.

This was the thing I ran to when things got hard. It was the thing that didn't judge me, the thing that always had me waking up excited, the thing that caused me to run away into seclusion, the thing that caused me to gain 60lbs and give up on everything else in life. It was the thing that got me to not shower for up to two weeks at a time, the thing that had me going to bed at 7:00 a.m. and waking up in the afternoon. This was an addiction. I remember finally breaking away from this addiction when I started losing weight, connecting with my dad, and living a real life. Then the temptation came back because it was still at my house. That is why when I cut something out of my life, I remove it completely from my environment. Your willpower must be trained, and quitting an addiction must be done cold turkey; it must be ripped away from you and your environment.

When I came back from a surf trip with my family and had 20 days off before going on another surf trip, I remember going back to my house, to the same room where I used to play games all the time, and I decided to fire up the computer. I remember just saying I was going to jump on for a minute and see who still played. That turned into 20 days straight indoors eating junk food and playing video games all out. It became a blur at that that point. Luckily, I had that surf trip planned at the end of the 20 days, which got me out of the cycle, and since then, I have never played like that again since I deleted my account. Our addictions as high-performing men will always pull us away from what matters most. My personality, which is like the personalities of most businessmen, is more inclined to doing something all or nothing, which can be used for good or bad. Now I channel my "be the best," "all in" personality to the values that benefit my life, and you can as well.

In the moment, giving up comfort and instant gratification is extremely hard, but know that there is always something better on the other side. If I didn't give up video games, fast food, and negative people, I would not be writing this book. Everything that this book will cause you to drop in life will only give you something better in return. It takes giving up the "good" feelings to discover the great. That is why we created the Three-Dimensional Businessman. That is why your example in the world is so important. There is a need for men to go out there into the world and gain massive influence and lead by example. It doesn't matter if it's one man with influence over eight million or if it's two billion with influence over four.

**"Your willpower must be trained, and quitting an addiction must be done cold turkey."**

# Do the opposite of the 99%

When I was 22 years old, my wife and I had a list of things we wanted in a house. It wasn't our dream house, but it was better than the 400-square-foot apartment in the east side of San Diego. It didn't have air conditioning, and in the summer, it was over 100 degrees outside. Our blinds were so cheap that you could see through them. It was the only thing we could get approved for, but we had a goal to only live there for six months. At that time, I was running my dad's carpet cleaning company and I had a job to clean someone's house that was moving out. It had everything we wanted in a house: a fireplace, an AC, a security system, two bedrooms, a two-car garage, a pool, a yard, and it even had two shower heads, which is great because Amanda and I made it a habit to shower together since we got married.

We were so excited when we heard it wasn't rented yet, so we scheduled a time to look at it together. When Amanda saw it, you could see her light up inside. The only thing was it was $450 more a month in rent. It was a great deal for the price, but that was a huge jump in rent for us at the time. But we knew that God has brought us this place since it was everything we wanted at the time. It also helped that the landlord, Dean Freeman, was an entrepreneur, and he believed me when I said, "Yeah we can afford this place. When can we move in?"

Dean was always coming over and giving us business advice. He was 72 years old and still did all the maintenance on the house himself. Every time he would come over, he would be giving us business advice and encouraging us to keep going. I will never forget his thick Southern accent he had when he told me, "Nicholas, there are three types of people in this world:

1. People that make things happen.
2. People that WATCH things happen.
3. And people that say, "What happened?"

### *"You are a man that knows that this life of success without sacrifice is for him."*

I'm daring to say that if you are nose deep in this book or listening to the audio, that you are the first type of person—a man who doesn't want to let life live him, and also a man that doesn't want to watch life from the cheap seats eating popcorn in the nosebleed section. You are a man that knows that this life of success without sacrifice is for him. A man that thinks differently from the other two types of people. The other two types of people are what we call the 99%. To be the 1%, it literally just takes being almost exactly the polar opposite of the 99%. When they go right, you go left. When they complain, we give thanks. When pressure comes, they avoid it and we press into it. When they think investing into themselves is a "cost" or "spending," we look at it as an investment. The way one-percenter Warren Buffett looks at it is that the #1 investment you can make is in yourself, hands down. If you are listening or reading this book, hands down, you are different. You are the type of man I would invest in. While others are on the couch, you are the man out there getting things done. So, give yourself a pat on the back, knowing that because you are the 1%. Now say out loud, "I AM THE 1%." Your bank account might not reflect it, but everything first starts in the mind. Remember, it first starts in the mind before it is a reality.

To shift that reality for you, I want to give you a gift, which is on the next page. It's our 3D Businessman screen saver that has our BDB Power Statement. Our guys print this off or put it as their phone screensavers. So, with this concept of a 3-Dimensional Businessman, you cannot have success with failure in another area. It will always catch up to you at some point in life. To digitally grab the

I HAVE A **VISION.**

I WALK IN **POWER & CONFIDENCE.**

I'M **EQUIPPED** FOR EVERY CHALLENGE.

I SURROUND MYSELF WITH THE BEST TO BECOME **MY BEST.**

I **VALUE** MY BODY, MY WORD AND MY RELATIONSHIPS.

I'M A 3 DIMENSIONAL BUSINESSMAN.

*Billion*
DOLLAR BROTHERHOOD

screensavers and all our resources. Go to www.thebilliondollarbody. com/group so you can join the The Billion Dollar Brotherhood Facebook Group.

# Your Daily Habits

The last thing that I've found to have an effect on success in every area of your life comes down to daily habits. When I got started in network marketing at 20 years old, I read a book from Darren Hardy titled *The Compound Effect*. He said in the book, "You will never change your life until you change something you do daily. The secret of your success is found in your daily routine." The problem I see in today's society is wanting the overnight success. The sad part is that people who have overnight success are lottery winners; they end up worse off than before they won. You don't want overnight success. Success isn't easy. It takes extreme consistency, and you have to focus on the right things. You might have heard this story, but let me ask you a question. Would you rather have a penny today that doubled every day for a month, or $1 million today?

> *"You will never change your life until you change something you do daily. The secret of your success is found in your daily routine."*

If you chose the $1 million today, then you are focused on the overnight success. If you chose the penny that doubled every day for a month, then you are focused on the consistent, sustainable success. The penny every day actually adds up to $5,368,709.12. When I first heard this story, I was shocked because my old self would have chosen the $1 million upfront. A penny doubled every day is kind of like your daily habits. It really adds up over time. Working out consistently for 90 days reaps big rewards compared to working out intensely for only 5 days. Writing down every day what you are grateful for will change your mindset drastically to focus on the positive and keep you from having down days.

Daily habits, though, can be overwhelming and are hard to remember. Maybe you have wondered, *Which habits are important? What specific habits do I need to do to achieve my goals?* As I told you earlier in the book, I'm not big on a 20-step morning routine. I want to be extremely productive, time efficient, and do things that actually give me a result. If you are anything like me, then you will enjoy the list below. The BDB Daily Rituals can apply to every single businessman because they focus on every area of your life, are simple to follow, and yield massive life results.

## The BDB Daily Rituals:

Become a Three-Dimensional Businessman, where you can have success without sacrifice.

## Health:

- Move your body physically
- Get good-quality sleep
- Fuel your body with healthy food and water

## Wealth:

- Write down the top 3 tasks in your business for the day and complete them
- Read out loud your Think and Grow Rich statement
- Read your BDB Affirmation

# Relationships:

- Journal and write down what you are grateful for
- Show someone you love that you care about them
- Add value to a growing relationship

The best way I have found to look at anything is to start at the ending. Meaning, what is it when it's done? Then work our way back to the very element. Some people call this reverse engineering. Kind of like the streets we see in America, with blocks and roads that almost look like perfect squares. I always say that I'm glad I wasn't in charge of that—I would have just randomly built without thinking about the end product, then I would wake up and we would have a big jumbled city. They started with the end in mind, then they worked their way backwards.

## Chapter 3 Action Items:

Evaluate and assess where you are at right now with the principles mentioned in this chapter.

1. What cycle of seclusion have you caught yourself in? Why do you think that is?

   _____

   _____

2. How can you break that cycle for good?

   _____

   _____

3. Which area of the 3D Businessman are you doing good at, and which areas do you need to improve upon?

_____

_____

4. What does it mean to you to "achieve it all" as a 3D Businessman?

_____

_____

5. Write down the best way to follow and stay accountable to the daily habits.

_____

_____

# THE 4 STAGES OF A BUSINESSMAN'S LIFE

For every man reading this right now, you are in one of these four areas: survival, stability, success, and significance. Living at my family's home before moving out of the house, I was in stability mode, cruising through life with just enough yet not really lacking much. As soon as I left the house, I felt the survival mode kick in quickly—living in a co-ed house with multiple people in one room, in a sleeping bag on the floor. I then later got married, and we started our first business in again a place of scarcity and got back to a place of stability, and then a place of success where we were making quite a bit more money than we were spending. Then swiftly our life took a turn again straight back down to survival mode, living off credit cards to survive, and I never truly knew why I was not living the life that I had dreamed about. It wasn't until someone broke this down to me that everything changed; they taught me about these four stages of life, and if you are just trying to get straight to significance, you will always fall short.

I decided to take the leap of going from survival, to stability, then stability to success, and finally taking the big leap to significance. I went from charging everything on a credit card to working in the family business, making enough money to provide while building skill sets to make the leap to success. I then refocused my goal on stability to a greater level of success when we launched out into our online business and built another stream of income. Yet I knew staying in this category would kill us because we were not money motivated, so if I didn't want to sabotage myself back to survival, I had to refocus again and make the quantum leap that we teach at our live events and to our coaching clients: significance. Taking the skills I had created, the drive I have kindled, I went all in on building the movement I had always dreamed of, and since 2016, it has been profitable, making an impact every month. Knowing where you are at, how to get to the next level, and not staying stagnant is something that has transformed the lives of the men we work with.

Figure out what category you are in, and what the next steps are for you to get to that next level to avoid the businessman's burnout where he creates problems that make his life fail over and over just to find purpose. There is purpose in reaching your full potential.

# Survival

*"My adrenaline pumped, I went into fight or flight, and there was nothing I could do about it."*

I remember getting a note saying that we had to move out of the place we were living in. We searched all over the place for somewhere to live. We looked at the places we couldn't afford and had to keep going back to the cheapest places on Craigslist. Until finally, we had a connection that linked us up with a safe way home for troubled children. They lived in a larger house, and there was a tiny one-bedroom house behind the property. We checked it out and we had to negotiate the deal because we couldn't pay the $750 a month. Our budget was $500, but we settled on $600 a month. This already was a stretch. We didn't know how we were going to do it. We then flew out that month to go visit Amanda's parents for the holidays, and during that trip, we went to an event to learn how to grow our business. During this event, we were motivated and excited, jumping all around because everything was in order.

As we were having a great time, I checked my email on my phone, and my heart started racing. I had no idea what to do. The email said that the state wouldn't allow anyone to live behind that house. Coming back from that trip, I knew we would have nowhere to live. As my wife looked hopeful, excited, and motivated next to me, I felt my stomach sink as I thought, *Shit.* The worst part was that I couldn't try to go solve the problem because we were out of town visiting her family. I had to eventually break the news to all of them as I had a life-altering moment. In that moment, I made a DECISION that I had to get from SURVIVAL to STABILITY! We arrived at Amanda's parents, where I pretty much ruined the holidays because all I said was, "I'm screwed, and I need to work." A normal thing for someone in survival mode, fight or flight, back against the wall, having to live on the edge just to make it.

We came back to San Diego, and I sold everything I had, and everything I enjoyed, including my motorcycle. We packed my stuff in the old room I grew up in. At that time, our network marketing business was almost at $0 since our whole team went to a different company. We also weren't very smart and got locked into a $550 a month BMW payment because we were young and wanted people to see the success. Oh, and we had driven up our credit cards because we didn't have enough cash to buy groceries. A month later, we found the cheapest 1 bedroom, 400-square-foot apartment in San Diego, where our carpet smelled like baby throw up. This was survival. I had to do something, so I started picking up work with my father's company. I was broke and defeated, fighting tooth and nail, feeling stress and pressure almost every moment of the day as I wondered when everything below me was going to crumble.

If you are in survival mode right now, you feel like you are going backwards and the momentum and currant are too strong for you to swim against. Many people in this situation still are trying to jump from here to significance by winning the damn lotto or looking for a handout. This is a place where you want to first jump to stability. This isn't an excuse to break your non-negotiable or let go of your dreams to be average. There is never a time for that. This is your time to break through!

# Stability

Stability is one of the most selfish places to live, and it causes men to become complacent. It's living at just enough for you and nobody else. This is where the majority of men live. To get out of stability, sometimes it takes going back to a feeling of survival to then make the gap or the leap to success. Stability can be the biggest burden— it's the valley where the Israelites wandered for 40 years in between slavery and the promised land. They say the walk from slavery to the promised land was only a 13-day journey, yet they wandered for 40 years! They were provided for and had just enough. This is one of the hardest places to live because it's really not "that bad." You could live here your entire life and be "fine." You won't be able to do any of the things you wanted to do, but you also don't have that fear of failing or getting punched in the face. This is that guy who has his business running smooth, or that job that is covering his bills. Squeezing by, just doing "enough." What a shame.

I started working for my father's business to ease the bleeding of my failing in business and producing wealth. I remember it all started just showing up to jobs just to help out, making $60 bucks here, a little tip there. I still have a picture that I saved when I first got a big tip! It was $50. I could really see this thing was going to take off for me. It's interesting that what we once hated can be desired. I learned this from carpet cleaning. I was cleaning model homes one night after hours—the ones that people would walk through all day and see which one they wanted built. It was raining super hard already, and I was just getting started. The hoses for carpet cleaning consist of a hose for suction, like a vacuum, and a solution line where the steam and mixtures of solution would run. All of the sudden, the solution line broke. I sat there in the pouring rain for HOURS trying to figure out how to fix it, only to know the reality of going back to work and finishing the job. In carpet cleaning, one of the most annoying things that can happen is getting a jet (where the steam comes out of) clogged. If it's not noticed, it can leave little streaks in someone's house from the thin missed spots. That night I sat there, and the only way I could know if this huge problem was fixed is if a jet got clogged. I ended up praying for the very thing that I despised in the past.

Stability can be that thing, and it is the hardest of the categories to move out of. When you drop into survival, you beg to go back to stability the way a homebody begs to go home when they are traveling. Stability is a step in the ladder, not a destination for a Modern Day Businessman. See, the happiness that we seek is not through stability; it's through progress—the constant forward momentum of growth in the key areas of our lives. Without this consistent progress, we are faced with the reality of having to create excitement through sabotage. We start creating problems to solve and become our own worst enemies.

# A man without vision will die

A key lifeline to a relationship, marriage, and a man's life is vision. Without it, a man dies. Today, it seems like most people are like zombies walking around—living for the day and floating around the currents of life, seeing where life will take them. There is a sense of unease because many people feel like sheep without a shepherd. Yet, if you go back into a time where there were more environmental pressures, you will see the importance of hope and vision. We live in a society now where we aren't concerned about starving, being attacked by a different tribe, or eaten by an animal. We as men had to have a strong will to live back in the day or we were dead. One example from the Bible was David. He went through hell, but because of his vision and God's protection, he carried out his purpose.

If you are in survival, the next step is stability. If you are in stability, it will take you utilizing the feelings of survival to jump, to then next steps of success.

Men are motivated by two key things: running away from something, or running toward something.

**"Men are motivated by two key things: running away from something, or running toward something."**

Running away from something: You wake up, you see your to-do list, and you start thinking about how if you don't do it, you are going to go backwards; and if you go backwards, you won't make money; and if you don't make money, then you can't pay your expenses; and if you can't pay your expenses, then everything is going to catch on fire and you will lose everything. So, because of that thought, you get into massive action! Utilizing the POWER of running away.

Running TOWARD something: The more positive side of the coin. You wake up look at your to-do list and start thinking about what life will be like in a week if you accomplish and check these things off the list. You look at the goals and rewards you have. If you hit your goals, you get excited about the future. The dream of what life could look like, the accomplishment would feel, drives you TOWARD something ahead of you.

Both are powerful tools to be used as a man pushes through the 4 S's.

# Success

What many men experience, but few stay! To stay in success, it takes the ability to produce! Success is where you have more than enough to do the things you want to do in your life. You are making more money than you spend. You are able to buy and do the things you love. You have the time to do what you want. The way you are creating income and what you are doing with your income isn't making a huge impact or difference in the world. This is the place where things start getting fun! Many people reading this are thinking, *Shoot, that sounds good! More than enough money to do what I want, and the time to do it! I am flourishing!* Hah, believe me, I think the same thing sometimes. Yet, inside this moment, there is still something missing from a man's life. This is a powerful step in a man's destiny and life because this is where a man learns the power of producing a result, keeping a result, and growing a result. No matter what, results that come easy are not good results. It's the ability to produce, keep, and grow results that brings power. What if we were to take a person who has been overweight their entire life, who has continued to become more overweight, and give them a fit body? Or a person who has been broke their entire life and continued to become more and more financially unstable a billion dollars? Or someone who has been in multiple failed relationships over and over and over again and give them the perfect spouse? What do you think would happen?

For most people, this would be the perfect storm! They would say, "Try me! I wouldn't mind having that problem…" Blah blah blah.

Men who walk in power don't expect something for nothing. If you give someone a result they don't know how to keep or produce, they end up going backwards in life, wishing that they never were given anything in the first place. If I were to give someone the results above, and they didn't know how to get that result, keep that result, or grow that result, they would end up going back to the same place that they were in before. Our lives and businesses will only grow as much as we do.

I was in stability working for my father—doing the carpet cleaning, carpet installation on the side, selling things on Craigslist, and trying to pick up a client here and there for our business. At this time of being in stability, I became complacent, hoping and wishing that somehow things would change and we would somehow get our big break. Expecting something for nothing. I started golfing a lot, finding my purpose through progression in an area of life that was easier and more rewarding. When I wasn't golfing, I would constantly play games on my phone to "process" after a long day at work. Meanwhile, my wife was waiting for me to get home, excited to see me, and waiting for me to step up as a leader. That time lengthened when I got a call one night. "Your father was in a motorcycle accident, and he is in the hospital." He didn't even tell me that he had crashed. I guess he jumped on a motorcycle, crashed with nobody around, woke up, got back on the motorcycle, and tried to ride home, jump in the shower, then get into bed. The pain was so bad that he had to call a friend, and they couldn't even get him out the door to the car and had to call the ambulance. He got to the hospital with his scapula in more than 30 pieces. His collarbone shattered in 16-plus pieces. His ribs were shattered. He had a collapsed lung, road rash on his face all the way to his legs, a bicep tendon detached, a torn rotator cuff, and a hernia the size of a ball in his stomach. Not fun stuff. And Dad, if you're reading this, that's what we call "running out of talent." Ha.

The constant problem for the man who reaches the success category without a vision for significance is that the dream of being successful ends up being better than the real thing. He can get whatever he wants and can buy whatever he wants but is not making the impact or walking in the purpose he thought he would.

He has made it out of survival and stability (which are the most selfish places to live), where he had nothing more than enough for himself, and now has overflow, is able to go where he wants, and is able to experience what he wants, but he needs something more.

# Significance

Significance is where most men and entrepreneurs want to end up, but they try to skip the steps to get there. This is the place where a man is working 100 percent in his destiny, making an impact through his company and life, making more than enough for himself and those around him, in a way where his life and things in his life are a walking transformation.

This man is walking in freedom himself, giving freedom away to those around him, and creating a ripple effect of success.

Sound like something you would want? I would hope so. Now let's identify where you are at on this scale. Are you in the survival, stability, success, or significance? Survival meaning back against the wall, constantly in fight or flight, with no predictable systems or processes in life. Life feels out of control. Stability meaning you're in a place where things are "good" because nothing really "bad" is going on. The bills are being paid, a small amount may be going into savings, and it's a place where you are able to take care of yourself. Yet to a man, progress = happiness and stability feels stuck. For men like you and I, this is where we would rather burn everything to the ground than stay stuck in this place. Are you in success? Where is your life? Are you in a state of abundance but lacking a tangible impact from your results—one where you can make an impact on others? Do you feel that you are not yet in the zone where you come alive? Or are you in the significance category, living a life that is a model of abundance and destiny? No matter where you are at, the first step is to accept that reality. Come to the realization of where you are at and OWN that reality. The next step is putting together a simple, controllable plan to get from where you are at to the next step.

*"This man is walking in freedom himself, giving freedom away to those around him, and creating a ripple effect of success."*

I remember walking into the gym for the first time at 19 years old with one of my good friends, Spencer. I had a vision of what I wanted to look like and the goal that I had. I remember how weak I was when I first started lifting weights—it was embarrassing. Week after week, I saw small improvements of strength and minor body changes as well. If I were to have gone into the gym and said, "Hey, man, slap on 315lbs for bench," I would have died. Though I had the vision of where I wanted to be, it took the constant progression of hitting small goals to get there.

There are so many men out there who have a lofty goal to do something like "be a philanthropist," yet miss the opportunity all together because they miss out on the steps to get there.

Like most, when I first got into business, I had no clue what these concepts were. I was firing from the hip, not using proven formulas and systems in life to see predictable success. I was completely broke with no job, just a lot of excitement and passions. I had lost 60lbs and ran into my first network marketing health product. It naturally just made sense since I could get behind it. After a year and a half of that, we moved on to starting our own health business, still riding on the expertise we had, our knowledge of the way we could apply that expertise to deliver value in exchange for dollars. Money in this world will always follow value, and value is broken down into solving bigger problems for more people. We packaged up the knowledge we had and the story we had created and sold it. We remember breaking 10k a month in that business, which was a HUGE goal of ours at the time, yet we knew we were not where we wanted to be and not doing exactly what we wanted to do.

## *"Money in this world will always follow value, and value is broken down into solving bigger problems for more people."*

I struggled in every area I teach about. I struggled with my health, relationships, and wealth in a way where I didn't even have one going for me. You will learn through this book that you can take your biggest mess and make it your message. I remember hearing a man named Tucker Max tell me that the best people to learn from are not just the people who made it easily due to chance, luck, or genetic giftedness. Also, it's not ideal to learn from people who have just failed, which there are plenty of those people out there. As I said before, most people want to give you their two cents, but it's only worth two cents. These are people who have experienced defeat, so they try to prepare you and teach you from a place of defeat. "I know you are going on that diet, but realize that if you are meant to be fat, you will stay fat." "I saw you were getting married soon... Are you sure you want to do that? I have been married six times, so you may want to think twice." Then there are the best people to learn from, those who had big oppositions, didn't have everything happen easily, but they still made it happen and became successful. They understand where WE are at and what we are going through and also know the plan to achieve success in that area. This is why people who are looking to lose weight typically will be more attracted to a trainer who had been through what they are going through and made it to the other side of having the energy, health, and body they want. No matter where you are at in the 4Ss, know that success alone is a joke—there is no such thing. Success happens with a formula of mentors, coaches, teachers, community, education, and application.

# Chapter 4 Action Items:

Evaluate and assess where you are at right now with the principles mentioned in this chapter.

1.  Which stage of the 4Ss are you currently in right now?

    _____

    _____

2.  What do you have to do to go to the next stage? What is holding you back from that?

    _____

    _____

3.  What are you motivated by? How can you use that to your advantage even more?

    _____

    _____

4.  Write down what your life will look and be like when you reach significance.

    _____

    _____

5

# YOU ARE YOUR #1 INVESTMENT: HEALTH

The value I had for myself was a direct result of how I treated myself. With no human investment, there is no human appreciation. Growing up, I didn't understand the concept that we teach today to gain power: the ability to create a result, maintain a result, and build upon that result. I remember when I was a kid I didn't know how much to eat, what to eat, what to drink, how to exercise, none of it. I felt like I was always expected to look and be a certain way without knowing how to actually create the result, which instantly made me—and, I know, others—feel messed up, jacked up, genetically screwed, and dumb.

My father was consistently doing physical labor and could literally eat whatever the heck he wanted and still look shredded. I got told that if you could "punch an inch" growing up, you were fat. I also got taught at a young age that when I was in shape (which I never knew exactly how it happened), I was praised, yet when I wasn't (which I also didn't understand), I was not. This led to me feeling insecure, self-conscious, and lacking a massive amount of self-esteem. If you feel or have ever felt ugly or fat, then you can relate. I didn't even feel comfortable taking my shirt off in front of anyone at a very young age because I knew I was going to get shit for it. I remember my dad coming up to me and punching the fat on my stomach, and it triggered me. I shouted out right away, "WHAT, ARE YOU GAY?!" I felt like I had to fight back with something mean since I felt hurt. That comment did not go over well with my dad.

When I was transitioning out of eighth grade to high school, my friend invited me to start wrestling. I knew my dad wrestled growing up, and it made me feel pretty badass thinking about it, so I started practicing with the high school team. This led to me getting into the best shape I had ever been in at the time. Of course, it didn't last. Have you ever seen depictions of the best football player in school, 20 – 30 years later, with a beer belly, resembling nothing of the glory days? I had reached a result through doing something that was not sustainable, and I didn't know how to keep that result. I remember wrestling practice being every day for three hours.

After I quit wrestling because of the depression and video game addiction, I was in gym class, and someone said I had gained weight. It was obvious that I was a lot bigger, but I didn't even realize it since I never wanted to look at myself in the mirror. I stepped onto a scale and I had gained over 21lbs of pure fat. They asked me what the scale said, and I lied. I said that it hadn't changed and I hadn't gained any weight. However, this reality hit me like a ton of bricks. It showed me again that pressure doesn't create weakness; it only exposes it.

When you are confident in an area of life, nothing that somebody says can hurt you. It's when they expose a belief that you have down deep that you can be triggered. This distant reality of confidence led me to summer school every year, avoiding my father because of my overwhelming realization that I was underperforming and embarrassed of how I looked. I came back to school that next year, and everyone was shocked right away about how much weight I had gained. I tried to shake it off but couldn't keep deflecting it. Some kid looked at me and said, "Nicholas, seems like it is a little nippily out today." I looked down at my soft shirt with moobs poking through it, and it cut me deep and formed another reality about myself. Rather than having the power to change it, I did whatever I could to hide it and cover up. I went to the mall and tried on sweatshirts until I found the exact one I liked. It wasn't a way to solve the problem but a way to cover it up. I felt my confidence coming back from it. But how could I cover up even more? How could I hide the embarrassment?

### *"When you are confident in an area of life, nothing that somebody says can hurt you."*

Looking back at what I did now is crazy. Once my mother came home and asked me, "Why the hell is there tape all over the ground?" I had to lie. What I was really using it for was too embarrassing to say out loud. I used it daily to tape down my nipples and moobs, finally taking it off when I got home, to only develop blisters from it.

It got so crazy that I only wore a certain type of underwear, which were stretchy, a certain type of pants, a certain type of shirt…all of them needed a logo to cover any definition. And the sweatshirt, that ended up being my dead giveaway.

115 degrees outside? *Naw, I'm not hot. I need my sweatshirt.* Burning up all day from the heat, nothing could get me to take it off. By the end of that year, the entire sweatshirt was faded from the sun hitting it. I wore it almost every single day. This led me to not wanting to see people or be around people at all. I threw myself into video games and became a complete addict. I was spinning out of control, self-sabotage in full effect. On the days I did have to visit my father, I would spend the entire night before not sleeping to then crash the next day and have to miss it. I would constantly stay up from Friday night until Sunday night each weekend, numbing myself through video games. During the summer, I would play 18 – 20 hours a day, drinking soda, Red Bull, and eating deep-dish microwave pizzas—to only hear my parents fight about how fat I was getting, which caused me to starve myself for attention.

# The Transformation

Now the reason I go in depth on this is to jump into the subconscious mind and show what billions of people are thinking when it comes to health, wealth, and relationships. To uncover what everyone is thinking but nobody is saying. That many of us are hiding, trying to cover up and putting on a masque of confidence.

It's only when we hit a breaking point, a wakeup call, a mid-life crisis, whatever you want to call it, that we actually decide to get honest with ourselves and to start living the truth. If you don't have the body you want, the energy you want, the emotional stability you want, then the first step is to stop covering it up and look at it for what it is. What is your current situation? Why is it that way? What do you need to believe to change it? What are the action items that need to take place?

The #1 thing that was holding me—and holds other men—back from accomplishing my destiny and having the family, relationship, potential, success, and EVERYTHING else in life stemmed from my health: mental, physical, emotional, and spiritual. This is where our confidence comes from. I believe that my body is a reflection of my internal world. So, once I started changing the things on the inside, my outward body start changing as well. Once I began to confront the truth that I wasn't taking care of my body, that I was covering it up and was not living up to my potential, then I started taking action. I found my motivation to change through the realization that I was underperforming in every area of my life because of my health.

### *"My Inner world creates my outer world."*
### *— T. Harve Eker*

I was a kid that always wanted to do big things with my life and be #1 in everything that I put my hands to. I just didn't understand exactly what to do. I needed a plan I could follow to create a result. By telling you my health journey, I hope you can identify somewhere within that. Maybe you have been embarrassed before of your body.

Maybe you're just insecure about your legs but you're shredded everywhere else.

Maybe you had a dad, a kid at school, or a different family member who bullied you and made fun of you.

Or maybe you're currently in the worst shape of your life and you want to change it. If you are, then keep reading because I will share with you how I've kept the weight off and have continued to get in better shape over the last 10 years.

# Your Image Matters

In my own journey, I've realized that I'm working on becoming the best version of me and making my external world reflect my internal. I'm 5'7" and built to be lean and strong, not bulky. I cannot compare myself to a completely different guy who has a different build than me and different genetics. I can only control my actions, not the outcomes. That's why executing on a plan and tracking is so important because if you aren't putting in the work then you will know.

As Three-Dimensional Businessmen, we have a responsibility to those who follow what we do because we lead by example. Some people say it in a frame of: "Be the man you would allow your daughter to marry." I like to say: "Imagine every decision is the decision your kids will make, or your clients." Think of it in whatever way it takes to bring the distant thought into reality. As an example of this, a family member of mine starting drinking beer at a young age even though they despised their father for being an alcoholic and drinking beer all the time. People don't do what we say; they do what we do. As a businessman, this means you a leader in your business, on top of your family, friends, and wherever else you are involved in. They are looking up to you as their example whether you believe it or not.

### "Be the man you would allow your daughter to marry."

One huge principle I learned is that people judge books by their covers. Like the cover of this book—that's why it's so dope because I knew you would judge it! I realized that how I treated myself showed the value I had for myself to the world. People judge us off first glance, and first impressions are everything. Throughout my journey, I found that simplicity was the key to success. That the best athletes in the world were the ones that didn't try complex things all day but were the ones that mastered and built upon the basics. Michael Jordan became a professional because he mastered the basics of basketball.

I discovered 5 physical attributes of health and have taught these to thousands of people. Here they are in order:

1. Breath
2. Hydration
3. Sleep
4. Nutrition
5. Exercise

Breath was shocking to me when I first discovered it because we are taught that the only thing that matters is eating clean and hitting the gym. However, it's not true. Think about it: if we hold our breath for too long, we die. If you are stressed, which business can often be stressful, you start to develop shallow breathing, which means you aren't getting enough oxygen. Not getting enough oxygen means you will have less energy, and this shallow breathing keeps you uptight.

So, in this chapter I will go over the five things we as businessmen can do every day to be healthy.

# Breathe

My favorite breathing practice is called Box Breathing. This is where you breathe in four seconds, hold it four seconds, release it four seconds, hold four seconds, and repeat. The "box" is four different four-second actions.

The second one is Prime Breathing by Tony Robbins, which you can find on YouTube.

A lot of yoga traditions have a focus on breathwork and being conscious of how you are breathing throughout the day. We can function with shallow breathing, yet it isn't optimal. You can change the way you breathe by creating daily reminders and habits—like deciding to box breathe at stop lights. It doesn't take long before the things you do consciously become things you continue to do subconsciously. The goal is it becomes less of a thought and more of your normal way of living.

I practice breathing in the morning when I pray, visualize my goals, focus on what I'm grateful for, and also when I work out. If you don't breathe when you lift, you could hurt yourself and you won't lift the weights as easily. Pregnant women even take breathing classes to help them get through the pain easier during labor.

A few benefits of focusing on your breath are:

1. Lowering stress, high blood pressure, and heart rate
2. More energy and mental clarity
3. Less anxiety
4. Detoxing

**Habit:** Focus on box breathing or prime breathing in the morning when you are getting ready and doing your morning routine. If you feel yourself getting stressed or upset, focus on deep breathing and exhaling. Stay conscious of inhaling and exhaling during your workout as well.

# Hydration

Did you know that while you sleep at night, you can lose up to two liters of water? Hydration is so important, and we can get it in multiple ways. Aside from drinking water, you can get hydrated through the skin, your breath, and food.

To create optimal performance, we want to make sure we have two things: the correct substances and the correct amounts. So first, I highly recommend quality spring or alkaline water, rather than the cheaper filtered water that you can buy. When it comes to your body, stick to the best you can afford.

### *"Drink more towards your full weight in water every day."*

We have heard this a million times: drink half your body weight in ounces of water. Many doctors and experts actually believe you should drink more towards your full weight in water every day. If you are active, drinking more water is especially important. There are obviously a ton of benefits of drinking water, but here are the main ones; you can actually notice a difference in when you are hydrated.

1. Your skin is hydrated
2. You have more energy
3. Your digestion is better, and you are less bloated
4. You have mental clarity, no brain fog.

I know drinking water sounds super easy, but if you are like me, you can easily get lost in work and forget to drink water. So, my key to success is always having a 32oz water bottle filled up all the time. I prefer a stainless steel one or a glass mason jar since plastic isn't healthy, especially for men. The plastics actually block testosterone from being produced. Dr. Anthony Jay did a whole podcast on the Billion Dollar Body about the chemicals that lower testosterone production.

Another thing I personally do is limit myself to one cup of coffee a day since it does dehydrate you, and I limit my alcohol consumption. If you drink a lot one night, you are gasping for water in the morning and your skin looks terrible from being so dehydrated. If I do want to enjoy 1 – 2 drinks out, then I make sure to drink two glasses of water with them.

**Habit:** Drink 30 – 40 ounces right after you wake up, then drink 8 ounces for every hour you are awake for optimal performance and 16 oz while you working out.

# Sleep

Sleep is a massive tool that businessmen can overlook because we tend to think it's not productive. I have been there, but once you know the benefits of getting a good night's sleep, you will start to prioritize more. It's proven that we can actually improve our skills as we sleep because we have a better memory. Sleep is a place where we file away belief systems as truths, put away thoughts, and get resolution on things. It's also a place where we detox our brains and boost our immune systems. Sleep has an essential role in having optimal performance and boosting our testosterone.

Genetically, some people can sleep less or more than others, so figure out what's right for you. Though it is the same when it comes to what you do before you go to sleep and after you are awake. There is a great book called *Sleep Smarter* by Shawn Stephenson that goes really in depth on hacking your sleep.

For myself, I like to unwind for 30 minutes before bed and wear my blue light blocking glasses if for some reason I'm on my phone. I drink my last cup of water with my supplements and magnesium to help me sleep better and then head to bed. I turn down the heat and make sure the room is completely black. I can get eight and a half hours of sleep most nights because working out takes more recovery time.

**Habit:** Set your alarm to go to bed. Then do a nighttime ritual so you unwind and relax. Make sure your phone is away from you and on airplane mode. Set the temperature to around the mid 60s and black out any light in your room. Aim for at least six and a half to seven hours of sleep.

# Nutrition

Nutrition is summed up by what you put into your body. There are three different macronutrients that all food can be categorized into: protein, carbs, and fat. Then there are micronutrients, which are vitamins and minerals. The key place to start is on what to avoid first. When I did health coaching, I would get a million questions like, "What plan should I do? Should I do paleo? Should I do keto?" My response was always, "The best plan to do is the one that you actually can stick with."

So many people get caught up in keto this, count this, or very restrictive diets. When I lost the weight when I was 17, I started out by eliminating the CRAP that I knew wasn't good for me. Once I cut the junk out of my diet, like processed foods, fast food, and many others, then I could add in the things that were healthy for me. I knew what to eat and what not to eat, but I wanted to know how much of each thing I should eat. Since I'm a "all in" type of person,

I weighed every protein, carb, and fat for four years and tracked everything that I ate. It all depends on what your primary objective is. I recommend eating foods that are not hard to digest for optimal performance and even doing intermittent fasting because digestion is the second most energy-draining activity. I'm not going to go in depth on ALL of the research I've done and tried, but I will give you the guidelines I personally follow. My good friend Christopher Walker has a great book called *Master Your T*, which has a lot of information around macronutrients, micronutrients, and lifestyle recommendations that help boost your testosterone as a man.

Here are 5 guidelines I follow when it comes nutrition.

1.  Eat 40 – 50% fat, 30% carbs and 20 – 30% protein. This is also known as the Zone diet.
2.  Eat or drink a lot of raw foods
3.  Stay away from fried foods
4.  Limit dairy and processed sugar as much as you can
5.  Eat organic, free range, grass fed, and wild caught foods 90% of the time. The 10% is for things I can't control of when I want to splurge.

**Habit:** Be aware of what you are putting in your body. If it's cheap and low quality, then you are saying to yourself that you don't deserve quality. Put foods in your body that give you healthy macronutrients and micronutrients.

*"Be aware of what you are putting in your body."*

# Exercise

This is the last of the five physical attributes. Depending on your goal, exercise can look different.

Most men are interested in boosting testosterone. High intensity interval training and heavy lifting are better than long-distance running or cycling. These will give you the biggest bang for your buck and increase testosterone naturally. Going back to nutrition, when people ask me the best plan to follow, it goes back to what you can follow and stay consistent with. I work out five days a week at the gym and usually do one other type of other activity like golf, basketball, skateboarding, tennis, cycling, surfing, or motocross. At some points in my life, I didn't enjoy going to the gym. I wanted to work out outside and do something fun, and so I chose sports instead. Please don't overwhelm yourself thinking you need to go from never working out to working out six times a week. Pick a goal that you can actually follow through on.

Below are a few of the benefits of working out, which you already know. One thing that most people don't talk about is that we as businessmen are high D's on the DISC personality test. This means that we actually let go of stress and process things when we do physical activity. If we don't, we get mad and stressed out. So, if you're feeling stressed, the best thing to do is work out and let it out. Working harder at your business will just make you more frustrated, but when you can hit a punching bag or crush a CrossFit workout, then you be focused again. Studies show that working out in the morning makes you more productive and focused. In 2008, a study showed the brain cells of the people who exercise on a regular basis have a higher brain growth rate. Incorporating exercise into our lives is a crucial part of being a successful businessman. It's time to make it a priority!

5 Benefits of exercise:
1. Increased blood flow and heart health
2. Better physical appearance

3. Decreased stress and anxiety
4. Increase of healthy hormones like dopamine and endorphins
5. Bone health and reduced likelihood of injuries

**Habit:** Write down your goal, pick a plan to reach it, and place accountability in your life to make sure you achieve that goal.

When these five physical attributes are followed, they are a foundation of success. If one is missing, then the structure will crumble. The investment in yourself is something that is constantly growing and never ending, from what you are surrounding yourself with, what you are putting into your body and mind, to what you are digesting and thinking, and what you are expressing, which is your actions and activities.

The last thing I want to include is external health. Your personal hygiene matters. Some guys take care of their skin, their hair, and the clothes they wear, and others don't. The guys who don't do this say it doesn't matter, and I have call BS on that. No one feels good wearing dirty clothes, smelling bad, and neglecting to cut his hair. Women love to have a man who takes care of himself and values the way he looks. However, it isn't just women. We as humans also trust people more easily when they look good and dress nice. As a man who wants to crush it business, our outward appearance does matter.

Here are a few things I do to keep up with my personal hygiene (which my wife has helped a lot with).

- I take care of my skin by cleansing, applying face masks, and moisturizing my skin.
- I brush my teeth and do all-natural whitening treatments.
- I make sure I'm clean shaven and have a haircut every two weeks.

- I style my hair.
- I ask for help when shopping and have a tailor to help fit my clothes to my body.

You might not need to read this if these are things you already do, but there are a lot of men who do not keep up with their personal hygiene and grooming, and it's not our fault. Maybe we just haven't been shown or we think it's girly to take care of our looks. If you're married, you can thank me later. If you're single, you can thank me later too.

Health and personal grooming give you confidence, longevity, and optimal performance. Without health, we have nothing. Without investing in our health, we are not Three-Dimensional Businessmen.

We are the lowest common denominator in our lives. We have the most power to create or destroy anything. We cannot accomplish 100 percent of our destiny, serve 100 percent, and give 100 percent energy and attention at 60 percent of our potential. We cannot give what we don't have. We must overflow as a man to be the change we want to see in the world.

**"Health and personal grooming give you confidence, longevity, and optimal performance."**

# Chapter 5 Action Items:

1.  What's one area of your health you feel insecure about?

    _____

    _____

2.  On a scale from 1 – 10 (10 being highest), how much are you valuing your health right now?

    _____

    _____

3.  Which of the 5 physical attributes of health do you need to focus on more? How can you make that a habit in your life?

    _____

    _____

4.  How can you upgrade your style or image to feel more confident?

    _____

    _____

5.  What is your health goal six months from now? Picture it, write it down, and create a plan to hit it.

    _____

    _____

6

# THE POWER OF MENTORS

My mentor Cole Hatter said something to me that transformed my life forever. Have you ever heard the quote, "It's not what you know, but who you know that matters"? I believe it's both—what you know and who you know.

Back in the day, what you knew was super powerful because whatever is in high demand or lacking is valuable. Everyone knew each other. You had to buy from the market; your family was from the same town for generations; everyone knew your mom, dad, sisters, brothers, etc. There was no shortage of people knowing who you were or who you knew. Yet information was a tough thing to find. You had to find some old person and trust what they were passing down was legit. Now information is everywhere, and almost everything you need can be googled. It wasn't always that way. I didn't have some Facebook ad hitting my feed giving me all of this information for free when I was trying to get healthy 11 years ago.

Now that there is so much info, we have to decide what information is the best for us and how to apply it.

### *Information + application = transformation.*

The shortage is who you know. With everyone going virtual, only talking on social media, in their homes all day, it's harder to have real relationships with people. So many people think the answer to their problems is in information; I used to think that way. But learning isn't just about your neural networks; your social networks have a huge, arguably larger, impact. My friend Jim Kwik is a learning and brain expert. He says that kids learn a lot quicker by who and what they surround themselves with, not what they consume. If you remember picking up habits or talking like your friend, it's because the people you around rub off on you. I still to this day will start talking like my mentors because I spend so much time with them.

I asked my followers on Instagram a question to see what people thought about the "what you know vs. who you know" statement:

### *"What would you rather have?*
    a.   A million bucks
    b.   Live with the richest person on earth for three years
    c.   50% chance at $200,000,000.00
    d.   A lifetime of travel

One guy said, "Well, the richest people have written a book talking about how to get rich, so I'll go with the money option." However, I don't believe that would be the smart choice. The most powerful part of being with the richest man in the world is not the knowledge about money that can be found in a book. It's about being around and in that person's environment and adapting to it! Being around the richest man means that his network and relationships now become yours. That right there is even more powerful than information. That story actually reminds me of Harvey Firestone. He was friends with Henry Ford, and guess what he created? Tires to on Henry Ford's cars. So, it's not that he was the smartest guy; he just knew the right people and filled a need they had.

*"Well, the richest people have written a book talking about how to get rich, so I'll go with the money option."*

# Mentorship Is Powerful

So, what is the difference between a mentor and another instructor, and why is it important? I believe that teachers teach you about a subject, coaches teach you how to maximize yourself in an area, mentors teach you about LIFE.

When I was 18 years old, I went to a men's only prayer group with my church, which was held every Tuesday from 5:00 a.m. to 7:00 a.m. One morning, I showed up and there was a man who I had never seen before. At the end of it, we connected, and he gave me a $1000 check to support my overseas mission work at the time. This started a powerful mentor relationship that I still have to this day. He is a Navy Seal who has since retired, but when I met him, he was still deploying and doing special operations.

He supported me during ministry school and even got involved in the network marketing company Amanda and I did to show that he supported us. When we moved down to San Diego from Redding, California, he had opened up a group fitness class in his background. Amanda and I jumped in full force, and for the next three years, I worked out with my Navy Seal mentor almost every day. During that time, I grew in my mindset and my physical capabilities. He pushed me, challenged me, and told me what I was capable of, even when I didn't feel like it. After working out, we would talk life and business since he was extremely smart with his money and investments. Jesse Itzler wrote a book, *Living with a SEAL: 31 Days Training with the Toughest Man on the Planet*, and it gives you a glimpse into what Navy Seals are really like. Most mentors won't be able to spend that much time with you, but Joost did that for me.

I remember Joost going on a deployment and while he was gone, I was hustling, cleaning carpets and going to a entrepreneurs meet up every other week. Every damn time I showed up, I felt like a failure knowing that I was cleaning carpets every damn day not really seeing the results that I wanted. One day, I decided to start dreaming. I started talking big game. That I was going to grow the biggest carpet cleaning business in all of San Diego. I was going to consult 10 carpet cleaning businesses to seven figures. Then when the economy collapsed, I would buy the failing carpet cleaning businesses and build an empire. Sounds pretty cool, right?

When Joost came home, I remember almost having the same moment I had with my dad a decade earlier. I told him all about my dream and everything I wanted to do. He didn't agree; he thought I should get out of it altogether, and then he said, "You haven't changed since I left." It hit me like a ton of bricks. I had changed my speech, yet I had not grown since the last time he saw me. Our paychecks grow, our reaches grow, yet in the areas we aren't applying ourselves, WE STOP growing. That was me, and the reality of that crushed me again. Except this time, I wasn't going to run away from that pressure. I was going to run into it. See, mentors are not there to tell you what you want but to tell you what you need. They are men or women in our lives who are living a life we can model because whoever you learn from, you get a piece of. Whoever you receive from in an area, you also get something of other areas of their life. A teacher teaches you about a subject, for you only to take the things that you already agree with and can confirm are true.

The problem with most men, especially old-school businessmen, is the reason they go into business is because they don't know how to sit under authority or learn from other people. They want complete control and don't want to listen to anyone. If people tell them what to do, they just do the opposite because they hate it. You cannot truly gain authority unless you are also under authority. You can't expect others to build your vision without contributing to others' visions.

If it was not for that moment of Joost calling me out, I would not be writing this book. That moment, tons since then, and tons before then have shaped my life. This moment got me to then consider building a business that made me grow and stretch. To then go meet with Gary Vaynerchuk and talk to him about my situation, where he gave me sound advice on what to do next. Without these mentors and counselors, we are like the guy who decides to find out that the world isn't flat but round again. We look over the ocean and think, *WOW, I bet there is land out there*. Rather than discovering what has already been discovered, it's our obligation to stand on the shoulders of giants. At BDB we talk about our ceilings in life being our floors. Our max potential is where we START to ensure the biggest results.

Here are the top lessons I learned from Joost:

1. Commitment is doing what you said you were going to do, even if you don't feel like it.
2. Be a man of your word and always follow through on things you commit to yourself and others.

3. Be excited when someone corrects you and tells you that you can do something. Always encourage constructive feedback.
4. When you feel like quitting, you have 40% left in you.
5. Live off of only 50% of your income.
6. Always be learning.

# The Power of Showing Up

High-level mentors and coaches have been a HUGE part of success for the top performers in the world, yet how do we create these powerful dynamics? This is one of the most asked questions I receive. I'm connected to a lot of great mentors and teachers. I can tell you that it didn't happen by accident; it took my intention first, and then my actions. I took action and invested back in the relationships that came my way.

### *"Fifty percent of success is just showing up."*

There is one common thing that every person has done to connect with a high-level mentor. That first thing is showing up. Like I said, my mentor Cole Hatter said, "Fifty percent of success is just showing up." The Amish used to say that when you start, you are already halfway there. There is power in taking action and consistently showing up.

Naturally, when you start dreaming big and are deciding that you are going to do something big, you start gravitating toward solutions and people that can help you get there. It's the power of what you focus on, you get. Think about cars; what is a car you constantly think about, or have ever wanted? Or maybe this happened when your family or you bought a new car. Every time that same car is in sight, you notice it. It feels like there are a lot more of them than before, yet it was because we were not aware of them. Like the old game punch buggy, where you would be able to punch someone if you called out a Volkswagen beetle; you never really notice them until you are playing the game. So, let's say you start trying to do this exercise with Ferraris or Lamborghinis… No matter how much you practice this in an area where there are none, you will not see them. Yet, when you head to Rodeo Drive in Beverly Hills, you would see more of these cars than you would in a lifetime in the middle of nowhere.

So, step number one is being aware of what you are looking for. Many of us have opportunities passing us every day because we are not aware; other times, we are aware, yet not in the path for opportunities to happen. We must be in a place for it to happen and be aware.

When I was 18 years old, I had my first encounter with this. I had heard about an influencer who seemed really amazing, and I wanted to make sure I connected with him. I had one friend that knew this influencer, so I let him know that I wanted to connect with him. Next time, my friend met up with him, he invited me to go along. I had to pack up and quickly drive two hours away to meet them for a breakfast that I couldn't even afford. I still don't know how I paid for my meal. During this meeting, I got to meet the influencer. I even drove him through Jack in the Box for an Oreo shake afterwards, and we exchanged numbers. Afterwards, I ended up driving my friend all around LA for the day and almost couldn't pay for gas to get all the way home. I only stress this because the people around you are like bank accounts; you cannot expect to have leverage with anyone if you don't first make deposits. You cannot withdraw from an empty bank account. I was constantly giving to have social capital and social equity in relationships.

A few weeks later, I ended up getting a text: "Hey guys, headed to go moon surf tonight at Trestles. Who is in?" I showed the text message to the friend I was with at the time. I remember all the thoughts that were going through my head: *There are probably tons of people invited. I've never surfed there before. I will probably look stupid. It's illegal to surf at night. What if I go all the way down there and don't even talk to the guy?* All the excuses in the world. The same excuses that everyone else goes through when the opportunity presents itself. My friend who was next to me in the car, who would have gotten a free ride from me, decided, "Naw, I'm going to stay behind. It's late, and it's going to be cold. Just too many uncontrollable outcomes." I decided to grab a banana and a protein bar, jump in my truck with my board, and drive in the night to Trestles.

I drove up there and realized something really quick. EVERY single person that received that text had those same thoughts that I did, and NONE of them showed up. It was just me and that influencer. Then he asked me if I could drop him off at the trail that leads to the beach so he could get down there quicker. Remember what I said about most leaders not willing to submit to authority? I decided to go drop him off, come back, park my car, and proceeded to skateboard down to the trail that I have never been down. I had to follow the people that were leaving the beach down the trail. I ran down the beach to the area where the influencer was surfing, when I noticed that there was one person still leaving the beach as it was becoming pitch black. They pointed me to the area to get in the water right before I paddled out over a bunch of underwater rocks. At this point, it was pitch black because it ended up being a cloudy night. It was supposed to be a moon surf session. I paddled out and got some of the best waves of my life with this influencer. We got to hang out, build a bond where he had invested interest in who I was. He then went in to go get a snack and I got stuck in the middle of the ocean in the middle of the night for five hours!

Towards the end, he came up to me and said, "Man, I wish you could come to the UK and Africa with us to speak and serve the poor." At this point, I was so amazed at what was happening that all I said was, "I will. I'll see you there."

That night proceeded with challenges. The police came down the beach, and I had to hide in the water so as to not get taken to jail or get a ticket. Finally, I made it in, tried skateboarding all the way back to my truck, and as I was riding, I was so tired from five hours of surfing that I ate it going down the hill. But I got back up, ran back to the truck to pick up the influencer while I was soaking wet, and drove him back to his car.

I went back home, and a few months later, what do you think happened? You could've guessed it. I showed up in the UK airport to say hello to the influencer and his team, without him even knowing I was going to be there. I slept on a floor in the UK, and then flew to Africa. We spoke to thousands of people in multiple cities together. Everyone else would have quit at some point, sabotaged one of those moments. Many of them wouldn't have even showed up, as you could see. Even years later, that same influencer got into tennis. He was always looking for people to play with at a snap of a finger. I kept showing up and getting my ass kicked over and over again, yet he knew he could always call, and I would show up; I got to continually connect with this influencer and build a bond by consistently showing up and not giving excuses, but giving to the people around me.

# Behind Every Great Man Is a Great Mentor

One of the greatest values of mentors is the ability to see ahead what others cannot see and to help them navigate the course to their destination. I've had phenomenal coaches and mentors in my life, and I have to dedicate any level of success I have to them. They are the ones that showed me how to shorten the gap to bypass their heart ache, money investments, all of it to go further and faster to them.

Mentors can come at a time when you least expect it.

When my father got in a bad accident, I had to stay back full-time and clean carpets while my wife went to an event with her mother. To be honest, I was kind of glad I didn't have to go; I was a nobody and didn't really like meeting new people at the time. She called me to tell me that there was a $5,000.00 package to buy at that event for a "mastermind," a place to learn and connect with other high-level entrepreneurs. She told me that she really wanted to become a part of it, yet they wouldn't allow her to buy it because we were so broke! They made her call me because they knew a husband would freak out if that went down! I knew my wife would never make a decision to hurt us, so I let her swipe that card. That card bought us our relationship with Cole Hatter and many others that we invested in for years after that.

### *Mentors can come at a time when you least expect it.*

Cole believed in us when we weren't making much money in our business yet. For three years I studied how he talked, how he spoke, and how he sold. I attended every one of his speaker trainings and did everything I could do get around him since he sold over 150 million dollars and spoken for 5000 hours from stage. Through his mentorship, I learned how to speak and sell from the stage, which has been an extremely profitable part of our business and given me the confidence to speak anywhere, anytime. In this instance, I went above and beyond to connect with him and learn. Amanda and I went to Las Vegas when he was there and would stay up till 2:00 a.m.

playing blackjack. I drove hours away to his TedX talk, showed up at everything I was invited to, and even went to his other business talks to watch how he sold from stage. This relationship changed my life, and he was living a life I could model. He was a family man who loved God and believed in giving back.

Here are a few things that I learned from him:

1. Make decisions based on you non-negotiable.
2. Give more money away and incorporate it into your business model.
3. Make your money work for you.
4. Sell by making people feel good, not by putting them down.

I then went on to investing $60,000 into Russell Brunson and his inner circle. I didn't know it at the time, but that relationship landed Amanda and I speaking at Funnel Hacking Live in front of 4500 people. I've done this with other relationships like Jay Abraham, Christopher King, and a few others, and it's always worth it.

Your life will always be transformed by the combination of WHO you know, and WHAT you know. You can work hard to build relationships with mentors, and you can invest. The best way to do it is BOTH. Relationships will ALWAYS cost you two things: time and money, yet it will always be worth it.

So how do you get great the high-level tactics along with the connections? For me, it takes in-person immersion to truly learn and build relationships. That is why I host BDB Live every single year and can confidently say it is the best event for businessmen. I wanted to create something that was high value, high connection and catered around what men enjoy. If you haven't checked it out yet, you can go www.BDBLive.com to learn more.

See, most people just see the successful people after they get their big break. They don't see the thousands of hours and years of heartbreak and fighting that built a foundation for a man. What is done in private will be shouted from the rooftops. So many people are concerned with how they look to everyone else in the public, while not making investments, while nobody is looking in the private times. People see Lebron James on the court, but they don't see him shooting and dribbling for hours a day. When you go all in on building up your skill sets as a man, it's something that nobody can take away from you. Nobody fears a man that knows 10,000 kicks, but they fear the man who has practiced one kick 10,000 times! That's what creates greatness. The mentors and people you surround yourself with are the ones that call out the greatness in you, show you the things that they have discovered to move you further faster, and not have to make the same mistakes they did. A wise man learns from his mistakes, yet a wiser man learns from the mistakes of others.

When you gain the skill sets to build relationships, network, and succeed in every area of your life, it's not leaving things up to luck or chance anymore. You have the power to duplicate those results over and over again because nobody can take away what you know. The best investment you can make is in yourself.

**"Your greatness is limited only by the investments you make in yourself."**
— Grant Cardone

# Chapter 6 Action Items:

1. Who are your mentors right now, even if they are just online?

   _____

   _____

2. How are you currently investing into relationships right now with either time or money?

   _____

   _____

3. What qualities do you want in a mentor?

   _____

   _____

4. Write down a few lessons you have learned from you own mentors.

   _____

   _____

5. How can you now be a mentor to other people in the area you are good at? How can you pay it forward?

   _____

   _____

7

# THE POWER OF BROTHERHOOD

Have you heard of the Congo? It's the third largest rainforest in the world. It has one of the most dangerous environments in the world in Africa. The average lion is about 420lbs in the regular areas of Africa, like the ones you have probably seen on TV. For every lion to live, it has to roll with a pride. Although, prides of lions stay clear of the Congo, and the most dangerous animal in all of Africa, which is the hippo. Something that has been shown to us as something nice and cute throughout our lives is actually one of the craziest animals in the world.

There is one pride of lions that has moved from the regular, more comfortable areas of Africa to an environment that is higher pressure, that calls them to play at a higher level. They are a pride of lions that have survived in the Congo. Because of their pride, they have been able to survive, yet because of their environment, they have become something different, something greater. These lions have become 150lbs heavier than any other lions and they have learned to do three things that other lions don't do. Because of the high-pressure environment that's caused them to level up, they have first learned how to swim. As you know, cats freaking hate water. The same thing goes for normal lions, yet these lions have used swimming for offense and defense. The second thing that they have learned how to climb tall trees for offense and for defense. The most important thing that these lions have accomplished together is really what I believe is most relevant. Something that every man reading this can relate to. They are the only pride of lions that hunt hippos, the most dangerous animal on the planet.

No matter what, even if a lion was 700lbs and could do all of that crazy stuff, it couldn't hunt hippos alone. A 400-pound regular lion also can't hunt hippos with a pride, yet this 700-pound lion pride can. So how does this story of lions and hippos resemble our lives? Well, every single man has a hippo-sized dream inside of him. Something that he cannot accomplish with a regular friend group, something he cannot accomplish alone, even at his fullest potential; he needs a pride, a brotherhood alongside them to fight, to defeat, and eat that hippo-sized dream. That is the absolute definition of brotherhood.

In the last chapter, I talked all about mentors, who are amazing, yet they will always be limited in effectiveness by the people and environment you surround yourself with. Everyone has seen a kid with a great mentor or coach that hangs out with dumbass people and does dumbass things.

- If you hang around five millionaires, you will be the sixth.
- If you hang out with five people who are alcoholics and who are doing drugs, you will be the sixth.

- If you hang out with five smart decision makers, you will be the sixth.
- If you hang around five depressed people, you will be the sixth.
- If you hang around five confident people, you will be the sixth.
- If you hang around five broke people, you will be the sixth.

It's inevitable. Who you associate with plays a big role in your results, or lack thereof. You need to think long and hard about whom you're spending the most time with, for wherever they're headed, so are you.

- If your friend is obese, you are 171% more likely to gain weight.
- If your friend is unhappy, your chances of being happy decrease by 7%.
- If your friend's marriage is ending, your chance of divorce increases by 75%.

When you eliminate negative people from your life, your life will drastically change. Then when you surround yourself with people who are playing a bigger game than you, the speed to which you grow, and your achievements, will skyrocket. I also want to point out that the things you read, listen to, watch, and feed your mind with are also a part of your environment. If you're like me, then you are all in or all out. So, when I got started on my track to success, I consumed success YouTube videos, listened to podcasts, read *Think and Grow Rich*, and only surrounded myself with people who were on the same path. I even moved so I live in a more prosperous-minded neighborhood.

Mentors won't always be in your day to day, but your friends and influences will be. As a new Christian, when I was 18, I was taught that what we look at, listen, and consume we then become. So, if you want to be more successful, healthy, and powerful man, then only consume things that will help you.

# You Aren't Alone

At a men's event a few years ago, one of the speakers told a powerful analogy about grapes, which is pretty relevant because I live in Temecula Wine Country. He said people are actually like grapes, which totally didn't make sense to me at the time until he explained it. He said that grapes grow in clusters, which if you've been to a winery, then you've seen them. Then he said: "It's physically impossible for a grape to grow alone. If a grape is growing alone, then it will actually be rejected by the vine and shrivel up into a raisin." We as men can't reach our potentials alone; if we choose to be isolated, then we will shrivel up and die. Just as there are grapes growing in a cluster, those grapes can be used for junk, or they can be used for a $500,000.00 bottle of wine. You get to choose the people you surround yourself with because the grape that is alone shrivels up and dies.

> **"We as men can't reach our potentials alone; if we choose to be isolated, then we will shrivel up and die."**

Another analogy that changed my life was about geese. I first heard this from a man named Les Brown that I met backstage at Cole Hatter's event. Many have heard the quote, "Birds of a feather flock together," yet this takes it to the next level. A goose that flies alone can fly 70% less distance than if he flies in a flock. So many men spend their entire lives flying alone, which is great if you want to move fast. If you want to go fast, go alone; if you want to go far, you go with a pack. I can only speak from my own experience of feeling like I wasn't good enough to be in a group of successful people and the limiting beliefs that I had no value to bring to other people. I was the lone wolf because of my own stories I kept telling myself. Once I got into a powerful community, a brotherhood, I finally gained the confidence in myself and was held accountable to my purpose and vision.

One of the brotherhoods that I have studied and admired are the Seal Teams. I saw was them move as a unit and support one another like I've never seen before. I was once listening to a Navy Seal do some Q&As, and he got asked: "How often do you operate without knowing exactly what you are doing it for?" I thought, *This is a great question.* He said, "That's a dumb question. There is never a time where the team goes in without complete clarity on the objective and why we are doing it and what our roles are." See, there is clarity toward one common vision and objective, or it's impossible to actually hit the mark. Again, this is a Seal Team for a reason; they could not accomplish this mission on their own.

As powerful businessmen, that already makes us different. We can't just connect with the same people who are okay with the status quo. There are people that don't understand us and what we do, and really, it's the opposite. With all the things we constantly have to get done, it can cause us to go into seclusion being the bird, grape, or lion that doesn't walk with a pride. It's because you were not born to be a junk grape, or fly with tweety birds, or be in a normal lion pride. You were born to walk with successful Three-Dimensional Businessmen.

I look at the movement of building brotherhood like a lawful, virtuous mafia. It's more than just a group of people. It's accountability; it's a standard that we hold ourselves to; it's a place where you can give without expecting anything in return; and when that is done over and over again, people's needs get met. One of the most documented "masterminds" or brotherhoods out there was between Harvey Firestone, Henry Ford, Thomas Edison, and Herbert Hoover. These men accredit their success to the bond that they all had together, with a likeminded vision that when they came together, it created what seemed to be a third mind or a mastermind effect that happened where there was a multiplication of sorts. These men from that went on to be inventors of some of the biggest advances in history. Henry Ford is a huge reason why we won World War 2 because of his ability to produce vehicles. His invention contributed to war vehicles like tanks. Not only that, he was the man who brought motor vehicles to the world! We have the president of the United States of America, Herbert Hoover, 31st President and American engineer. Lastly was Harvey Firestone, the one that I really enjoyed, because deep down for me (whether it is correct or not), I picture him being the one who wasn't really that creative, but he was in the crowd. He saw that Ford was building these cars with these rubber circles, and he also saw that they kept wearing out over and over again, so he decided to create the solution to the problem by creating Firestone Tires, which we still see all over the place today. These men were amazingly talented in their own right, yet they knew that if they wanted to accomplish more they were going to have to work together, stick together, and form something that we now know today as brotherhood, which is similar but more tangible than a "mastermind"; it's proven that the concept is clear and works.

Growing up, we cannot control the environment we are born in, yet we can control the majority of everything else. A lot of us grow up and we make friends around our neighborhood, the daycare we are in, the school or activities we are in, etc. This was me. I grew up and I remember meeting kids around me, meeting kids at camp, meeting kids at school, and other people who played World of Warcraft. I always looked up to the kids who were impressive and seemed to have potential or were extremely liked, yet I didn't see myself as worthy around these types of people. The first time I had moved schools was in between fourth and fifth grade, and I had to make a new friend group. The majority of kids who I was hanging around those days were breaking rules and setting an example that I was following because of my association. If you looked at where they were going, that's where I was going. It wasn't until I spent some time with a friend that I hung out with in the past who seemed different that I started to understand. It seemed like something inside of him had changed, and I could tell. I even tried pushing his buttons and trying to make him slip up because it felt so weird to see him go against the grain. See, as businessmen and as leaders, it's our job to create waves, not just ride them—and this guy was creating them. This naturally led me to want to connect with him more, so I started hanging out with him any chance I got until one day, I was hanging with a deadbeat at the time and I decided to call him and see what was up. That's when he introduced me to the best man at my wedding and two other legit, evolving people. I used that one connection to connect with another completely different group of friends. I constantly pulled that string until I kept rising higher and higher. I felt more and more disconnected from the unmotivated, unmoved, and the passionless.

**"Growing up, we cannot control the environment we are born in, yet we can control the majority of everything else."**

I was so consumed with growth and purpose that I almost puked at the thought of my friends just hanging out and watching TV at night because it wasn't accomplishing anything. You are 100 percent in control of your friends group and the people you surround yourself with. You cannot control what environment you are in, yet you can control staying there. I constantly kept leveling up myself like that first friend did and took the motivated with me. I didn't have any hard feelings about the ones that were not motivated; it was just the best for both of us to not be around each other all the time. That doesn't mean we can't say hello or do something together occasionally.

I have a mission and vision that requires people who want to attack life with everything they have. This is why wealthy men invest in country clubs, unique memberships, join car clubs, live in nice neighborhoods, and work at great companies because they have mastered association. There is a capital and equity that is even more powerful than money, and it's social/human capital. Still to this day, I am pulling at that string to consistently surround myself with Henry Fords, Herbert Hoovers, etc. Some of the best ways that I have done that is by making large investments to be around the best and be trained by the best. There is a quote that says, "Rising tides raise all ships." When we are in a powerful environment with people who have a likeminded vision, we can accomplish more than we ever thought was possible. Whatever that community honors and gives attention to increases. Meaning, if you have a brotherhood like a gang, the things that are looked at as positive or good are stealing, killing, destroying, etc. So, it will drive a person in that community to naturally do those things because that's how he'll get attention, recognition, and status. Yet, if that same person was to get into an environment where GIVING was the way to get attention, recognition, and status, then naturally, he would start doing that. I experienced this first hand with a mastermind I invested in with Cole Hatter. Giving was a huge message in the mastermind, and it made me realize that if someone had a good heart and wanted to give, then great. But if someone didn't care about giving, but all they wanted was recognition, status, and attention, the only way they could do it is from giving. So naturally, even if someone was 100 percent selfish, they were still doing the right thing and actually could make a bigger impact in someone else's life than the person that cared.

When it comes to being a Three-Dimensional Businessman, a Modern Day Businessman, it starts with you. The people around you will see the transformation and want to become a part of the mission, and when you are surrounded with these types of powerful men, you start adapting to their environment and start doing things that make you superhuman because they are the things the community honors. There is a common thing in movies where the women never like their husbands' or boyfriends' friends. Women want their man to be around other good men. A woman will never be happy or fully trust you if you are hanging out guys who are cheating, doing drugs, and are disrespectful. The likelihood of you doing those same things is extremely high. That is why women love what we do in The Billion Dollar Brotherhood and at BDB Live. They want their man to be around good influences.

Getting outside your current comfort zone and mindset of what's possible will change your life. It takes raising the perspective to go to the next level. It takes getting out of that small ass pond and jumping into the ocean. When I'm in the middle of the United States, the "fit people" look like regular gym people on the west coast because of the perspective. They could be the best in their gym, yet the worst in California. Relationships, family, and wealth are the same. When I was 20 years old, I thought people that made $10 – 20k a month were gods. I was too scared to say hello to them, to approach them. A few years later, I met a man that didn't eat food until he made $10,000.00 for the day. Being around that man shifted my perspective and expectations in life. When we consistently up level our pond, we grow. We go from the guy that was making $1,000 a month in a $10,000 a month pond, to the guy making $100,000 a month in a $1,000,000 a month pond, and so on. You know you are in the best environment when the people you surround yourself with are better than you, and you are the worst in the room. When you are the best in the room, you are the loser of the room and are getting the least amount of benefit. Shift your community; shift your perspective; shift your outcome. If you are the loser making $500,000.00 a year right now, don't worry, you will still be a loser when you get a new friend group. I would just rather be the loser making $50,000,000.00-plus a year around people who are doing a lot bigger and better things.

> **"Getting outside your current comfort zone and mindset of what's possible will change your life."**

IF you're ready to up level your environment and discover the power of brotherhood, then I invite you to join The Billion Dollar Brotherhood. We have a free Facebook group you can search for and ask to join by filling out the three questions. This is where we add value to each other, build connections, and help each other hit our goals. There are also more ways to get involved by joining our virtual mastermind, attending BDB Live, or applying for BDB Elite, which is my inner circle of businessmen.

# Chapter 7 Action Items:

1. What are the things you consume and deal with that are negative? How can you eliminate them from your life?

   _____

   _____

2. On a scale of 1 – 10 (10 being highest), how would you rate your current environment?

   _____

   _____

3. If you had a Brotherhood to support you, how much more successful would you be?

   _____

   _____

4. If you have had trouble connecting with men before, what limiting belief of lie has kept you from it?

   _____

   _____

5. Where actions can you do to up level your pond?

   _____

   _____

8

# TRAITS OF A SUCCESSFUL BUSINESSMAN

For greatness to be found, there has to be an example. Something we fully aspire to be. It's one thing to be accepted for where you are at. That is a huge step to building community and growing. Anyone who doesn't accept people where they are at usually ends up pushing people away. The next part that so many people crucially miss is that they leave them there. It's usually either one of the two, or black and white. Either they accept you where you are at and then don't hold you to a higher standard and push you to become better, or they only hold you to a high standard and don't accept who you are to be able to walk out of the transformation. Throughout my journey, I have run into a ton of people (really every person) who are doing things that I wouldn't approve of in my community or in my environment. Yet there are a few factors that come into play. Everyone has heard that ignorance is bliss. When you don't know something, you are less accountable when it comes to doing it. Yet, when you know something, you are now held accountable. With great knowledge comes great responsibility.

As you read what characteristics a powerful businessman embodies, you may find some and think, *Hmm, that's interesting. I never knew that.* The only problem is now you do, and now you are held accountable to what you know. When I was growing up, I always ate junk, and a lot of times overate. When I was young, my dad could always eat a lot, and it seemed like it was something cool, and that I should try to one up him. I was overeating without the education that it was bad or going to make me overweight. Then when I figured that out, I had to make a decision and become accountable to what I knew, or it would eat me from the inside out.

My standard of the people that I will work with or talk to isn't for them to be perfect and believe all the same things as I do. It's strictly that they understand where they are at and they have a vision to change and improve that reality. The people that I very rarely surround myself with are people who are doing something that is not beneficial to their life and they don't want to change it.

Without a standard, there is nothing to shoot for; there is no way to reach human potential. I recently did a spin class with my wife because she loves doing spin. You show up, they give you shoes, you clip into your bike, and on the bike, it shows you the power you are pushing at, the RPMs and the resistance you are using. Throughout that class, they fully accept people where they are at, even if they cannot keep up. Yet, they have a standard of where people should be and should be shooting for to know they are successful. Rarely will we ever see greatness without a standard. Like in the Olympics, if someone posts a really good time or score, the next person knows that they need to beat that to succeed, so they will do more and be more in that moment.

I strongly believe in having standards that are impossible to ever reach or be in your life, while fully accepting the process to get there. You will never fully achieve being a 3D Businessman. There is no human currently alive that will ever experience perfection because perfect is measured in our own eyes. It's the heart and willingness to work on growing every day that is what we are after, not perfection. I couldn't understand this reality at 13 years old when my father said I would never be the best. He simply knew that I would never be happy if that's the only thing I wanted and expected because you can't be the best every day, or for a lifetime, at something. I had to have both of these beliefs hanging in the balance.

# Commitment

The first thing that a successful businessman embodies is commitment. The ability to do what you said you were going to do after the feeling you said it in is gone. Commitment is not something that is exercised during the "feeling" of motivation or inspiration. The point of commitment is to decide, then do it even with the lack of feeling. Literally using feelings and logic together to make a decision that your future unmotivated self will follow to produce a favorable outcome.

> *"The first thing that a successful businessman embodies is commitment."*

The gym is a great example. The majority of times that I go to the gym, I don't feel like it at all. And without a true commitment, I may allow that feeling to win for a few days. Then finally, I go to the gym, even though it sounds terrible, only to leave happy and excited that I did that. Feelings in the moment cannot be trusted because commitment would have got me in the gym and to the real feelings of happiness sooner. A man who lives his life with a lack of logic and feeling will always fail. Feelings and logic are meant to get you to make a commitment, so when they are not there in the future, you still do the best thing to produce the favorable result in your life to experience true success.

What do most people do? Most people out there consistently make commitments and never follow through on them. They make commitments to others and break them, and then make commitments to themselves and break those even more often. Here is what ends up happening: we actually start to lose trust in ourselves because we keep quitting. This creates a cycle that is hard to break. One of the biggest commitments we can ever make is marriage. Think about what we say: "In sickness or in health, for richer or for poorer, 'til death do us part." Those are some big commitments when you think about it. A commitment that over 50 percent of the US population breaks every year. So, if over 50 percent of people break this commitment, then what happens? Well, statistics say that over 90 percent of those people will actually end up getting re-married again—except with a 15 percent higher chance of getting divorced again. See what happens when we break a commitment, big or small: it's not going to prevent us from committing to anything ever again; it increases the chance that we will break our commitment the next time.

It's easier for a man to make a commitment and keep it when it's with someone other than himself. Back in the day, commitments were kept through handshake. Let's say Tommy made a commitment to Joe that they were going to meet under the apple tree at 3:00 p.m., and they shook on it. The commitment meant something. Generally, both parties would be more compelled to show up because they didn't want to let each other down. Think about the last time that you made a small commitment to someone else, even if you didn't follow through on it. Were you more compelled to follow through on it because of the other person? 99.9 percent of the time, the answer is yes, though that is not the most important time to have commitment and follow through. When you break a commitment to a person, they have less trust in you. Though Tommy made a commitment to Joe and showed up at 3:00 p.m., think about the last time you made a commitment to yourself and you didn't follow through on it. Let's say it was, *I'm going to go to the gym today at 3:00 p.m.* Nobody in life has the intention to never be fit. We generally have a commitment or goal that we give up on and never fulfill. It's a lot easier for the majority of the world to break the commitment they made to themselves rather than everyone else. This creates a total mind tangle because the conscious mind and subconscious mind are at war. They don't trust each other, and therefore you build a lack of trust with yourself. When your conscious mind makes a commitment, your subconscious calls BS because it's heard that one before. The worst person you can break a commitment to is yourself. Build trust with yourself by making small commitments and following through on them.

My Navy Seal mentor taught me more about commitment out of anyone I know. We used to create workouts, and sometimes we'd get through part of a workout and decide it was a terrible idea. Yet he taught me to finish the commitment that I made, then afterwards, I could decide whether I wanted to make that decision and do that workout again. So, we were more intentional with our commitments the next time. These two different days really solidified it for me. One time, I was doing a workout and I saw a Navy Seal face plant on the street, tripping over himself running (just because they are badass, doesn't mean they are always coordinated). When he fell, I remember watching the Olympics where a runner falls and everyone helps them finish, so I tried that. He was so confused with what I was doing, so he just told me to keep going and didn't care. He ended up finishing the workout while bleeding, then cleaned himself up. He knew that deep down that instance sucked, but what would suck more is training himself that when things happened, he didn't have to finish his objective.

The second one was an even simpler task. Joost was walking his dog, and one of the cameras on his house caught him jumping on his skateboard, going off the curb of his house with his dog, falling and smashing his face on the ground where his face was physically bleeding. He simply got up, jumped on his board and kept walking his dog, came home, and then washed up. His training made his actions simple; it was a way of life at this point to make a decision, finish it, then move on.

> **"Commitment means to do what you said you were going to do, after the feeling you said it in is gone."**
> —Nicholas Bayerle

# Consistency:

The second trait of a successful businessman is Consistency. Tony Robbins says, "It's not what we do once in a while that shapes our lives, it's what we do consistently."

I lived in Redding, CA for a few years, which is about 11 to 12 hours north of San Diego. Regularly, for holidays and such, I would have to drive down and back up to come visit. I learned something so profound from those trips that represents the majority of people in life. The majority of people in life are the rabbit in the tortoise and the hair analogy. If it was just me headed down to San Diego, I would jump in my truck, go just above the speed limit, and cruise my way down the freeway with as little stops, sightseeing, and distractions as possible. I would have people constantly blowing past me on the freeway going close to 100 mph, and I would sometimes think, *Man, I wish I had the balls to break the law and go that fast.* Yet what would happen? Five to six times throughout the trip, they would blast past me going 100 mph. Every time they would gain ground, they would stop here, stop there, get food here, grab a snack here, go to the restroom here. Even though it seemed they were going so quick, with all of the stupid distractions, I would end up beating them to San Diego because a lack of focus and consistency.

The same thing often happens in the gym. Someone will jump in the gym and workout hours and hours for a short amount of time, get distracted, then end up around the same as where they were at, except with a lot of wasted time. Whereas, when you put on muscle and maintain a healthy body fat percentage, your body naturally wants to keep itself that way. The longer you maintain healthy levels in your body, the easier it is for your body to sustain that; yet, when you end up going up and down, the body ends up not making true gains. Maybe you have been a yo-yo dieter before or someone who does a 30-day challenge but then goes back to your old ways. You know the feeling of never making any consistent progress.

So many men sabotage their health, relationships, and their wealth by lacking consistency. Consistency also builds trust with yourself and the people around you. If you know someone who switches products and businesses regularly, what's the thing that everyone says when they do it again? "Oh, another one of those things." Yet if that person was consistent for a year, they would build trust with those around them to finally get on board. A lot of opposition in people's lives is actually because they lack consistency, so nobody can actually ever back when they do, and when they are not backed, it makes them switch what they are doing again to only create a vicious cycle of being a chronic quitter. If you were to work out hardcore for 90 days, you would see a great transformation indeed, and if you didn't do any exercise for the next 90 days and ate junk, you would look like crap. Easy come, easy go. It's better to have consistency to create longevity and the multiplication factor. The only way for a businessman to truly succeed is to have consistency.

# Ownership

The third trait is ownership. Without taking 100% responsibility, a man will always be a victim, unable to change his situation.

A man goes on 10 dates. Ten of the girls break up with him. He makes 10 investments, none of which are profitable. He tries, fails, and blames it all on every girl, every investment, every person who talked him into it, every circumstance, like a damn Tasmanian devil. The lowest common denominator in every man's life and every situation he is in is himself. If you ever go to an Alcoholics Anonymous meeting, you must first confess where you are at; if you don't admit you have a problem, nothing can change.

One of my mentors once told me about how he had saved up $250,000 dollars in over a decade's time, and he decided to go and invest in real estate with some big players. He flipped them his $250k investment, they threw in their investment, and the deal failed. They went on doing more deals, and he was crushed with his entire life savings gone just like that. He had many decisions to make. He could complain about the deal, complain to all of those guys, give up on investing, blah blah, blah, or do this. He taught me about this concept of "accepting your reality quickly." It requires a few things.

1. Figure out exactly what happened.
2. Take 100% responsibility for what happened.
3. Accept that reality fully.
4. Figure out how to improve from there.

He constantly told me that so many people get attached to things or ideas. He had to tell himself, "I had $250,000. I lost it all, it's my fault, and I accept the reality that I'm now $250,000.00 less rich. How can I improve from there?"

### *"Take 100% responsibility for what happened."*

Before I could quit the carpet cleaning business, I had to take ownership of where my income was at and realize that I'm paid on the value I provide. I needed to gain a skill set that was valuable so that I could make more money. I took ownership of where I lived, what I was able to give my wife, how my body looked, and everything in between. No one else caused me to have these results; it was me, myself, and I.

There is a great story about being three feet from gold that shows ownership in a different perspective. There was a man named Harby, and his uncle was searching for gold. He started digging and actually ended up finding a vein of ore. Back then he couldn't just text his friends, so he covered it up and returned back to his house to raise money for the equipment that he would need to dig it out. So, Darby and his uncle went back to finally strike gold and live the life they wanted. They actually ended up finding a good amount of gold and paid off their debts. Next was on to the profit! Yet the gold stopped appearing, and the vein that they thought was going to make them rich disappeared. And it was not for a lack of digging; they kept digging and digging but ended up with nothing. They then gave up and ended up selling the equipment to a junk man for a few hundred dollars. The junk man called in a mining engineer, who also took a look at the mine and found out that there was a vein of gold just three feet from where Darby and his uncle stopped digging. That junk man ended up making millions just from that one mine.

Darby learned a valuable lesson; he went home, paid back all of his debts, and lived with that lesson for the rest of his life. Whenever you feel like giving up on your dream, remember that you may be just three feet from gold!

When I have told this story in the past, the majority of people think, *Wow, what an idiot that guy must have felt like.* They all embrace the victim mentality and focus on what it would have felt like to lose that much and fall that short of victory, not knowing they do it every single day. They just complain that it's everyone else's fault. If Mr. Harby were like those other people, he would have been depressed his entire life because he had an opportunity, banked on it, and it didn't work out for him. It would have caused him to live in a constant state where he was not able to move past it. He would have never made it to phase two. The thing that is not told in this story was about how he had to move on, accept his reality quickly, and figure out how he could do it differently next time.

He left, and though he stopped three feet from gold, it was the best thing that had ever happened to him. He made a million a year in his next profession of being an insurance salesman, recouping all the money he would have made from the gold mine and gaining so much more. Ownership is taking someone from a victim and transforming him into a victor; taking someone who thinks the destiny of his life is out of his hands and the world is going to control him, like a ship lost at sea with to rudder with the wind and the waves, to a man that has power to take 100 percent ownership and control of his life. This is a place where he takes responsibility because that is what is expected from him as a leader. It's taking someone from a pauper and making them a king. A king rules over a kingdom. If someone does something stupid in his kingdom that he is not even connected to, guess whose fault it is? Not the stupid person; it's the king's fault because it's his kingdom. Same goes to the man who is a CEO who has someone in the organization who makes a mistake; he takes responsibility because it's his organization. Same for the man of the house—whatever happens in his house is ultimately his responsibility, and so is how he reacts to it. And if true for those areas of life, how much truer for the things he actually does? Ownership is the beginning and inception of power—it's the starting point. Today, take 100 percent ownership. If it's meant to be, it's up to me. Figure out from this place how you can move forward.

# Focus

**"Obsessed is a word used by the lazy in order to describe the dedicated."**

A few years ago, someone had the pleasure of sitting down with both Warren Buffett and Bill Gates at one dinner table and that person asked them a serious question. He asked, "What is the number one thing that attributes to one's success?" Interesting question, right? One that would call you forward. An answer that could literally shape someone's future. What's crazy is Bill Gates and Warren buffet actually had the same exact answer: "Focus," or as some define it, "follow one course until success." So why is focus so powerful, and how can we use it to our advantage?

Whatever we focus on in our life increases and builds desire. We then attract the things in our life that we are constantly thinking about and talking about. If we focus on avoiding junk food that we are craving, we end up sabotaging ourselves to eat it and get it over with because that focus builds desire and obsession. Being a motocross racer and really into anything that has wheels, one of the first things you learn when racing is if you are trying to avoid something, for example, a rock, most people would keep their eye on it because they want to make sure they don't hit it. That sounds correct until you actually experience at what happens. When you focus on the rock, you actually naturally gravitate toward what you look at. So rather than FOCUSING on the thing we are looking to avoid, we focus on what we are looking to go toward because not only will we head that way, it builds an immense desire.

One thing I love about entrepreneurship is that hard work beats talent when talent doesn't work hard. The guy who is less talented but obsessed and wants it more than the other person will more than likely win because talent can only take someone so far. *Think and Grow Rich* explains this concept in relation to money. That the only way to get it is to become completely obsessed with money where you couldn't imagine not having it, where you put your focus on what you want daily until you get it. Focus builds obsession, and obsession builds urgency.

Everyone knows that I raced motocross growing up, but few know that I actually picked it up again after Amanda and I had been married for a year. I couldn't afford a bike, and had not rode in years, but I decided to start watching the sport again. After I started watching the sport, I started studying it and building a desire to ride again out of my focus on the subject. For somewhere around nine months, I watched up to five hours' worth of film every single day, trying to immerse myself in the sport; since I couldn't afford to ride yet, I wanted to make sure that my brain would think and move the way that the professionals did. This built such a deep desire and obsession inside of me that I could start crying at the blink of an eye. This caused me to outwork the other guys, who were even local professionals at the time. I outworked them in the gym, I rode more than them at the track, I studied more video, and my vision was clearer, which caused me to surround myself with the best possible to create growth and progress where they had plateaued. Many men experience obsession but never master it through focus.

About a year after I finished high school, I left for ministry school. At that school, there was a family of Australians, some of the most amazing people I have ever met. They had this crazy big, advanced espresso machine and showed that they were 100 percent serious when it came to making coffee. I was so uneducated at the time; all I knew about coffee was the quick machines that would make it, throw a couple creamers in, and BOOM, that's the best coffee you could ever have. I remember going up to Peter, one of the top Baristas in Australia, and feeling like such an idiot when I think back to it because I totally didn't understand the art and craftsmanship he put into what he was doing. He had coffee grounds all around him, and I was shocked! How could he just let those sit there? He said they just allow them to go to waste and don't use them because after 10 minutes, they have gone stale. I had only ever bought ground coffee, so I tripped out and thought to myself, *Shoot. You should give those to me!* He didn't use creamer or sugar in any of his coffee either, so it was really confusing. Yet the coffee was different and amazing, so my friend and I asked if we could stop by again soon and try his coffee again.

I had an espresso machine at my house that my stepmom had given me before I left for school. I started taking it a little more seriously when I would make myself coffee every morning. I started watching him when we went over there, then finally I asked him if he would train me. He had to serve coffee by himself to everyone on Sundays, so he agreed, and I started helping him on the Sunday afternoons. Because of the focus on the craft, it became an obsession of improvement to the point that if the family wanted coffee in the morning, they would ask me if I wanted to make it. I would drive over there just to use the machine and materials and make them coffee. Which then led me, after Amanda and I got married, to take ALL of the money we got from our wedding and a little more and buy the same espresso machine they had.

I would buy 10lbs of coffee every single week and make coffee out of my house and just practice and practice. I would wake up every morning, excited to get out of bed at the thought of making coffee for my wife, and often make her coffee that was by her bedside before she woke up. I would practice coffee the majority of the day, serve at garage sales, and even got to the point where I paid a coffee shop, Intelligentsia in Los Angeles, to train me with everything they knew for $150 an hour. Literally paying a place that would employ me to teach me instead. THIS is obsession. This led me to, in a very short time, becoming one of the top 1 percent of coffee makers in the world.

I then fell into this same thing on accident with golf, a simple process where I started studying it, building desire, playing the sport, practicing, and seeing the improvement. I was constantly looking to grow in my game, watching the best of the best, surrounding myself with people who were always better than me. In a year's time, I went from shooting in the 120s to shooting in the mid-70s. Focus that then became obsession resulted in me hitting golf balls seven days a week, seeking massive improvement, and surrounding myself with the best. See, so many people play golf their entire lives, hardly ever get any better, and keep playing with the same damn people they have always played with.

## *"To be successful as a businessman, FOCUS is needed."*

I use focus in everything we do in Billion Dollar Body—when we do a launch, put on a live event, come out with a book, or whatever we are working on. We know that having one common goal and objective is needed for success. That is how we've been so successful over the last few years.

To be successful as a businessman, FOCUS is needed. The ability to stay true to something long enough to become a master at doing it. This was the constant thing I never understood. It's very easy to get addicted to improvement, yet at some point, you stop progressing as quickly and you hit the law of diminishing returns. When you constantly keep working at something, you end up getting smaller and smaller improvements. I always thought I was just undisciplined and uncommitted. I had quit at school, quit in motocross, quit at skateboarding, quit at coffee, motocross again, golf, business—everything I had done at the time, I had sucked at. Then my mentor told me something huge, and he said that it was okay that I quit those things. They were passions, not responsibilities. As men, we can get caught up in passions or addictions. You may feel the most passion towards a television show, a video game, women, drugs, sports, whatever it is. To be successful, we have to channel that energy through focus toward something that is a responsibility, not just a passion. It's okay to move on and quit something you are doing for fun or doesn't line up with your future. Use focus and obsession to maximize your results in your priorities.

# Giving

Every successful businessman gives more than he takes from any and every situation. The principle and power of giving was one of the first principles I encountered as a man. More blessed is the hand that gives than receives. It's also the only time in the Bible, Malachi 3:10, that God himself says to test him. So, I decided to do just that. I decided to go on $8000 worth of trips, serving the poor with no income at 19 years old. I kept a list of the money I made and the money I gave. I made $20 and I gave $8. Then I made $30 and gave $12. The numbers kept rising until I had to start a bank account, and finally, I went on those trips and came home yet still needed to pay my mom back for more than $2800 that I told her I had yet couldn't charge any more money on my card. I still remember looking at my bank account with $550 dollars in it and I decided that there was no way in hell I was going to pay my mom back with that money. So, I decided to take 100 percent of all that money and give it away. Two weeks later, I walked into my mom's house with $2853.50 cash and coins.

I had not yet learned how to work, yet I did discover that in life we sow, and then we reap. As a businessman it's our moral obligation to leave this earth giving more than we take from every situation. It's a way to experience prosperity even in the hardest moments, to give even when you do not have enough because you know that prosperity is your future. To invest your time into people, your money, to not be attached to things that most people would be attached to because you know there is an overflow and abundance in these areas. I have taken this principle with me into business, not just because giving money helps other people or because it comes back to me but because the simple act of giving keeps your heart, mind, soul, and spirit in alignment. This alignment puts you in a position to prosper in all areas. Modern Day Businessmen continue to give even when it's uncomfortable because it forges us as men just as much if not more than it helps the people we give to. This isn't the most logical principle, yet maybe that's why God says to test me in this.

### *"Modern Day Businessmen continue to give even when it's uncomfortable."*

As businessmen with employees, we should be giving. As business owners with clients, we should be giving. As brothers, we should always be giving. As husbands, we should be giving. As sons, we should be giving. As fathers, we should be giving. It's not always giving our money that matters but something that is even more important, our time.

When I sat down with one of my friends and mentors, Russell Brunson, we talked about how tough it is in this world to find mentors you can fully look up to. He talked about how the last thing you want to do is get to know your heroes because when you get to know your heroes, you realize that usually they are not heroes at all. You start seeing the good, the bad, and the ugly of what every person goes through. This is also a huge strength as a businessman to know that the biggest thing that you can be is transparent with who you are. Because no matter who you attract into your life, you will have to continue being that person to keep them. Most people act like one person in a certain environment and then change in a different one. That's not us; that's not a Modern Day Businessman.

Throughout all the years, the only man I have been able to 100 percent follow is Jesus and the works that he has done. The way he spoke, the way he captured attention, gained influence, and created a movement. He's been my biggest role model; the standard he set is the one I push myself to live, even if I have to accept reality for where I am at. He set the highest standard I know for any man and calls us out to follow it. I also gain a lot of wisdom from the other areas of the Bible. John C Maxwell is one of the best leadership teachers, and he gets everything from the Bible—how to lead, how to parent, how to be a good husband and friend; the list goes on and on.

# Chapter 8 Action Items:

1. What commitments do you have right now? How can you follow through on your commitments more?

   _____

   _____

2. How can you create your goals and use the power of focus to hit them? What distractions can you eliminate to help you do that better?

   _____

   _____

3. What are your responsibilities as a man?

   _____

   _____

4. Write down a few instances you have taken 100% ownership. What area of situation in your life can you take more ownership in?

   _____

   _____

5. Write down 5 values you have and want to embody even more.

   _____

   _____

# WHY BUSINESSMEN FAIL

*"Whether you think you can or can't, you're right."*
— *Henry Ford*

I had the honor of interviewing my mentor Russell Brunson, and I asked him what has made him successful. Was it the hard work? The mentors? He summed up everything it takes to accomplish what you want in life in one word that rocked me: "Belief." He said he just believed it would work. He believed it was possible.

I remember hearing a story once of a boxer named Buster Douglas; he fought Mike Tyson and actually got knocked down in the fight. He was just about to get the 10 count when the bell rang, saving him from losing that round. Not one person up to that point had been knocked down by Mike Tyson and ever won. Buster went back to his corner and got ready for the next round. Everyone expected Mike to come out, guns blazing, and knock him out. So, the next round started, Mike came out smelling blood, and something crazy happened: Mike got knocked out. Everyone wondered what the heck happened. Buster's mom had told everyone that he was going to beat Mike Tyson before she died, and two days before the fight, his mother died. He went into that fight with a different belief because he was fighting for something greater than himself and it gave him a bigger "why" than Tyson.

Did you know that most of what we believe to be true is created by the time we are eight years old? That's where we build all of our beliefs, our confidence, and how we view the world. If we are experiencing a constant negative belief or trait, we usually always have to look at our childhood and get to the root cause of it. I recently went through some EMDR (Eye Movement Sensitization and Reprocessing) therapy and got to learn about why I had a fear of being alone, a fear of people leaving me, a fear of abandonment, and other self-limiting beliefs. The answers were all found within my upbringing. So, if you have these negative beliefs, don't try and think your way out of it. Let go of the ego and seek professional help to really get past these roadblocks.

Ultimately, our belief systems shape who we are. Everything external manifests internally. Our current belief systems actually put a lens on how we see the world. Our perception of the world creates our reality, not reality itself. One hundred people can look at the same event and see something differently all because of the lens they see life through. To change our results in life, we have to first change the lens in which we see from. Yet the majority of lenses are created before we are eight years old, then manifest throughout our lives. Even when we deal with things that happen when we are 20 to 30 years old, until the lens is dealt with from the root, it will still operate in our life.

Some of the more extreme cases of this is what we would call child brain—where a man gets triggered by a trauma that happened in his past as a child. When he gets triggered, he actually starts acting like that child that he was that age; it takes control of him and makes him do stupid things he regrets later. An example of this is when he is disrespected by someone or his wife and his anger takes over. He then hurts the people he loves and once he calms down, he regrets it. These are the more serious issues and can be very common with high D personalities in men. There is a great personality test called, DISC. High D personalities are dominant, competitive people. Getting professional help is highly recommend if you want to live a fulfilled, successful life.

There is a great verse, Romans 12:2, in the Bible that says: "We are transformed by the renewing of our mind." That is why personal and spiritual development is the key to going to the next level as a businessman. Tactics and strategy can only take us so far when we have a mindset issue.

There are the three main areas to transform a mindset.

1.  What you ingest: The things in your environment—what are you watching, listening to, reading, and surrounding yourself with.
2.  What you digest: What are you thinking about and contemplating, chewing on.
3.  What are you expressing: the actual actions that you are taking because of your thoughts.

This single handedly was one of the biggest foundations that I developed in my transformation of being a Three-Dimensional Businessman. It was the seeds that I planted that grew trees that didn't bear fruit for years but are doing so now. I believe every man has to go through this to win. We cannot change our childhoods, but what we can focus on is what we can do after that. As you know from my childhood, there was what was happening, and then there was my perception of it. That's why when you bring things up to your family, they usually don't remember what you are talking about because they didn't see it as a "big deal" when it happened, though we feel like it was.

### "We cannot change our childhoods, but what we can focus on is what we can do after that."

Some of my main core beliefs were established between the ages of two and five. When I was two, my father pushed me on a bike, and I became the youngest person in the world at the time to start racing bicycles. That was a positive experience that brought out competition. Then one of my first negative experiences (outside of family) that I had was when I was around five years old. My brother had a friend, a girl who was probably only 11 or 12 years old at the time, and we were playing hide and go seek. I was living in an apartment complex with my mom at the time and decided to hide in a dryer. I remember sitting there for a really long time and started to wonder what the heck happened. So, I jumped out and realized that they had just left me. Something inside of me shifted; this was a pretty girl, who had more influence on me because of that, and she basically left me and didn't care. I got so angry, upset, and bitter that I wished I could just hit her. I remember grabbing a wooden bat and running toward her but could never actually hit her. Now I realize this was also after I was in daycare when I was an infant until age two because my mom was in school. Then I was in preschool when I was three and four before going to my first year for school. So, at this point, deep down, I had already felt alone and was struggling with massive anxiety. These experiences can make us or break us depending on our outlook. Many more things happen that we don't notice that end up shaping who we are, some for the good and others for bad.

I was with a close family member, and at the time he was lying in a bed, I went to go sit down on the bed and have a chat, and when I did, he flipped out and tried jumping out of the bed. I was so confused that I had no real thought of what could have happened. Me being me, I got intrigued and started poking around at the situation, wondering what the heck happened. His instincts told him that I was going to try and trap him in the bed.

1. Why would I ever do that?
2. Why the hell would it matter?

See, our brains will always protect us and go to survival mode, and it takes discipline in the mind to win at life. This man was claustrophobic—a person who has an extreme or irrational fear of confined spaces. Realize everyone has stuff; it may not make sense to you, but it does to them. This man had an incident when he was younger when people would pin him down and tickle him until he couldn't breathe, which then manifested into claustrophobia. Some fears keep us from dying, but the majority of them keep us from living. The only two fears we are naturally born with are the fear of loud noises and the fear of falling. Every other fear is a learned fear.

These are the common things businessmen struggle with internally. Notice the ones that you can relate to.

- The fear of failure

- The fear of being rejected
- The fear of not being enough
- The fear of success
- The fear of what people thinkThese then produce self-sabotage, codependent behaviors, feelings of unworthiness, low confidence and self-esteem, depression, anxiety, toxic relationships, dishonesty, putting on a mask to make other people happy, total isolation, and many others.

### *"Transformation requires a continuous daily practice of renewal."*

There are millions of symptoms out there, all with core root causes, all with core traumas or beliefs that have been built through experiences, upbringing, and society. So, again, let's focus on the right things. This idea is something that will constantly need to be renewed. You can't just renew your mind once and be perfect. Transformation requires a continuous daily practice of renewal.

There are two types of extremes you should avoid.

1. Thinking that you don't need any help and can figure it out all by yourself.
2. Navel gazing—where you only focus on all of your problems, thinking that when you are "fixed," you can start.

Both are bullshit. The goal is to see problems and focus on the solution. We are all humans and are going through similar journeys. Once we can open up and share the things that we struggle with to people who are like minded and can help, we start becoming free. It's easy as men to think we need to be strong 24/7, but sharing our struggles and feelings *is* being strong. Women don't have as a hard of a time sharing the truth and opening up. There are many books about the psychology of this, one being *Men are from Mars, Women are from Venus.* When we can let go the ego go, we then grow. Our mess will then become our message, but we first have to overcome the mess.

In earlier chapters, I talked about how what you do in private is shouted on the rooftops. What that means is you have to put in the work in private to then be recognized by the public. Towards the end of high school, when I had just lost 60lbs and got my first six pack, I realized there were things missing from my life. I tried going to a few parties with friends, tried hanging out with the wrong crowds, and it made me feel uncomfortable and out of place. That then led me to trying to figure out if there was a bigger purpose out there. Not many people know, but that actually led me to buying Ouija boards, with good intentions at first. We, of course, wanted to see if there was anything bigger out there, and we started out looking for "good spirits." We became impatient and started just calling for the bad spirits to speak to us. If you've ever seen a ghost/scary movie, then you have seen this type of spiritual activity before. This led me to a seven- to nine-month path of staying up all through the weekends and doing this stuff. The spiritual world became very, very real to me during this time, and I found myself bound in fear from that. Remember when I said we become what we focus on? That is exactly what happened to me. The kids at school called me "Demon Kid." This was a dark place for me, trying to find my purpose. That was a mess that would soon become a message.

However, living that type of life and going after that stuff led me into fearing for my life and the lives of everyone I cared about. I knew I needed to find the light. I eventually reached out for help from a Christian kid I knew. He invited me to a prayer group, and this led me to having an encounter with God. That one moment changed my life forever. I knew there was a God and I felt like a completely different person. I went home, prayed over my house, got rid of the boards, and stopped talking with my toxic friends. I knew that I had to change my environment immediately.

Our past has so much power over our future, and I discovered a system that has worked for me and that others have used as well to overcome stinking thinking. When I got out of high school, I started going to community college purely because I had no clue what to do. The majority of everything I had done up to that point was to gain the approval of my dad or others. I decided I was going to do something different; I decided to drop out of community college and take nine months completely off. Every day, I would wake up, and starting at about 8:00 a.m. I had my own school—reading a book, reading the Bible, meditating, worshipping, and praying. This was my silent time that I knew would be shouted on the rooftops, yet my family and parents had no clue what I was doing. This was a time where I truly knew I had no motivation from outside people, that it was purely internal and not for the approval of others. Nobody had any clue what I was doing or why I was doing it. Yet I knew all along what it was preparing me for…something big. Those nine months transformed my heart and my mind.

One of the first things I looked at in my life were the two extremes. Most families have things that they pass down from generation to generation that are good and bad, some of those are built through experiences and beliefs passed down through the family. Those were the first ones that I wanted to make sure went to hell. So, one of the things that I would do in prayer would be to search for those beliefs, experiences, and triggers that I had on the inside of me, so I then could be reminded of the very first time that I ever had that thought or experience. Once those were identified, I could go back in time with a new understanding as an adult and gain total clarity from a new perspective. I would even ask for God's eyes to show me exactly what I was supposed to learn and gain from it. As I was doing this, I was almost filing away experiences, breaking free from traumas, and understanding why I had those limiting beliefs. It was like taking shackles off my body and experiencing true freedom. I started to feel like I was walking in a new level of power. See, everyone's trigger has a core belief like we talked about above. This isn't a symptom; this is a belief that creates the symptom. Cure the symptom, and it just changes; cure the root, and it stops growing.

### *"Cure the symptom, and it just changes; cure the root, and it stops growing."*

So, I constantly did this every chance I got and also practice it today with the concept that pressure doesn't create weakness; it just exposes it so we can see it and deal with it. I kept diving into a bad or false belief that would be shared with me, dive back to the very first time I experienced it, and as I grew, I started to find out that there was a core belief there at the bottom of all that, that becomes a lens that we see life through. The goal is to then replace that core belief with the truth or positive belief, and to hammer that into your way of thinking and gain a clear understanding of what had happened.

A while back, one of my friends was in South Africa speaking at an event about disciplining your children. In one example, he talked about how you hit a kid on the fanny for discipline. He noticed everyone looked shocked. He found out later that fanny meant vagina in South Africa. His heart was pure, his intention was good, yet because of what people thought about the word and their understanding, they got something completely different from what he was saying. Based on our experiences, upbringing, and culture, we gain lenses that we look through, which end up producing the most powerful statement there is: the I AM _____ statement. These statements are only valid in my life if they can last eternity. Most people's beliefs are situational. Like I AM COLD. Great, if you get a damn blanket or turn on the heat, you will not be cold; you will be hot. Then there are beliefs like I AM DUMB. That core belief will drive you into the ground. It's not positive; it's negative. It's something that creates a limit on your potential, so that's how I know it's a lie. The truth to that lie is I AM SMART.

My wife once spoke with a phenomenal therapist and discovered her core belief deep down through experience is that she was dumb, no matter how many degrees she got, she still thought she was stupid because it was a powerful belief, not a reality. Same with body dysmorphia, where people see themselves as fat even though they are fit. Most people focus on statements that are negative, limiting, or don't last eternity. The goal is to replace them with the ones that do. I AM POWERFUL. I AM VALUABLE. I AM WANTED. These are the core beliefs you want to have in yourself.

So, when you are going through life, you can make declarations or search them online to find things you can say daily to give yourself power. That's a great place to start, yet when you feel pressure and it exposes a weakness, it is the best time to dive deep to figure out when the first time you experienced that was, what the core belief is. Then you must replace that and create a new belief, and that new statement is your declaration until you have full belief in that reality. Again, everything comes down to belief; whether you think you can or can't, you're right. I attribute everything that I am doing now, and that is being shouted from the rooftops, to those nine months of pure, uninterrupted discovery and growth, which I may never get to do again. So many people want a "FEELING" of breakthrough. Yes, when that happens, that feels great. Yet there is no real feeling when you plant a seed and are waiting for it to grow. You plant the seed of transformation, keep that belief alive by watering it with what you think about, surround yourself with, and act on, then reap the harvest of the fruit that comes from it. Remember, take things to the ROOT, the core belief, the core moment, and uproot it from there. For some, it may take coaching, therapy, or guidance. Church may be the place for some of you and a safe place. For others, you will go after it like I did. Depression isn't a condition; it's a symptom. Suicidal thoughts are not a condition or a belief; they're a symptom. Lack of self-esteem is a symptom; lack of confidence is a symptom; lack of belief is symptomatic of an underlying lie that is believed. Until it's addressed, consciously or subconsciously, no matter how many times we try to sugar coat shit, it's still shit. Allow your heart, mind, and soul to be renewed by healing physically, spiritually, emotionally, and physically. Smash limiting beliefs in the face and take your life back. Gary Vaynerchuk talks about going to someone you know and asking them to tell the truth about you, your strengths and weaknesses. I believe every person should have someone they can communicate with and bounce how they are feeling off of to get the correction they need when it's needed. This is a never-ending process because every day brings new pressures. This life is not meant to be walked alone. Transform yourself by renewing your mind and heart.

**"Transform yourself by renewing your mind and heart."**

# Chapter 9 Action Items:

1. What is a "limiting belief" you know you have? How has that shown up in your relationships and business?

   _____

   _____

2. When did you first experience that feeling? Can you pinpoint the childhood experience that led to that belief?

   _____

   _____

3. What is the truth? What do you want to believe?

   _____

   _____

4. Now write down a few statements you want to embody more of and put it somewhere you can look at every day.

   _____

   _____

# THREE ELEMENTS OF A SUCCESSFUL BUSINESS

As a Businessman, you know the risks involved with building businesses. The stats show that 90% of businesses fail in the first five years, and 99% in the first 10. The majority of businesses in the world are just exchanging a service or product for money, dealing with customers instead of clients. A customer is someone who buys a product, service, or commodity. A client is someone who is under your protection, meaning that you care about their success, not just the money they are giving you. Throughout my time studying businesses and people, I have found that people will buy a product and stay for the community, what that company stands for, and how it makes them feel. You yourself are actually a walking business. Whether you like it or not, you are constantly creating what is called a personal brand. This personal brand has a story, a value that it offers to the world, a way it represents itself, and so on. Whether you are looking at yourself and more of a personal brand, or if you are looking at a business in depth, these core principles work. One of the hardest things I've seen entrepreneurs go through is they keep chasing shiny objects and jumping from one good idea to the next. Maybe you have been there before; I know I've had these distractions. You could even get to point of growing a business and then feel burned out. That feeling is normal, and almost every entrepreneur goes through it. Some businesses and ideas sound exciting, then after you get into them, they are not. Have you felt this way? I know I have, and it leads us to thinking there is something better out there. Some people end up finding their passions and what they really want to do. I believe that if two equal people with equal potential come together and one is extremely moved and passionate about what they are doing, that person will win.

So, what is the difference between a goal and a why in a man's life? How do we push ourselves to superhuman limits?

Here is an example of a goal. If I were to ask you to walk on a 2x4 piece of wood for 100 feet that was placed on the ground for $500, would you do it? For me, hell yeah, I would do it. I would take that money like I was taking candy from a baby. Thank you, come again. Now, let's say I take that same 2x4 and I put it between two buildings that are 100 stories high, same exact thing you have to do, yet just a 100-story drop to your death. Would you do it for $500? What about $50,000.00? There is always some idiot that says, "Yeah, I would do it." Cool, call me and I'll set it up! What's the reason we don't do it? It's the same exact thing that we did on the ground, just higher up in the air. The reason is the risk is higher, and that's where we realize that money is just a goal; it's not a good why. Many people have their why's jacked up, and it enables them to actually take action.

Who is the person you love the most? Okay, now that you have that person in your mind, let's do this again. You are 100 stories high and have to walk 100 ft across on a 2x4 piece of wood. Except this time, it's not cash on the other side; it's the person you love the most calling out to you, begging for help because the building is on fire. You are either going to go over there and try to save them or watch them burn. Would you do it now? Hell yeah, you would. Why is that? Because you found a WHY, not a GOAL. They are not the same thing. A why will always give us a one up on the competition and give us freedom, hope, and excitement.

### "It's just as much about you as the leader as it is about the business."

After years of studying wealthy people and businesses big and small, successes and failures, short term and long term, I came up with a concept that revolutionized our business, my personal life, and will affect every business I am involved in going forward. It's just as much about you as the leader as it is about the business. It's called the Three-Dimensional Business. Usually people have one of the three dimensions or even two, just as most businessmen are not yet Three-Dimensional Businessman. Having one or two dimensions does not create a sturdy foundation. Assuming you already know what you are looking to get out of your future and are making steps towards it; assuming you know what you are particularly good at and what you are weak at to make sure your focuses are in the right place; assuming you have explored the areas and ideas that you have for the business you want to go into and the value they will bring into the world, this is the chemical X or the secret sauce.

The first dimension is creating a mission and vision that is bigger than a product or service. For years, I created a product and would go out there and try to sell it to people, chasing after the people instead of having them come to me. Equally, after I would get the purchase, they had no reason to stay in the ecosystem. On top of that, everything got boring to talk about. It felt like I was stuck in a corner, only talking about the product or service and nothing else. I realized something was missing.

So, what is it? It has nothing to do with your product; it has everything to do with the big problem you are solving in the world. See, you get paid based on the size and quantity of problems you solve. That is basically the definition of value, solving more problems for more people. Money will always follow that value. So, as a business, we took on a bigger identity and decided we are going to redefine what it means to be a businessman, literally change the dictionary definition. That if you are not prospering in health, wealth, and relationships, you are no longer a businessman. We are creating success without sacrifice through a thing we call brotherhood. Nobody in the world will live without hearing this concept, and we will know we are successful when we create 3D Businessmen who not only live this life themselves; they actually influence others to do the same. When we started talking this way, having a future-based cause, a mission and vision that was bigger than a product or service, all of the sudden, being someone who stands for something became easy. And talking and promoting the company became easy because anything that contributes to creating Modern Day Businessmen was fair game! Now did I say how? Nope I didn't. I'm enrolling the right people into a mission, and the reason everyone who wants to be in on it is because even the guy on the bench wins a Super Bowl ring. They want to be part of something big. Most people don't have a vision for their lives, so when they see someone who has a clear one, they want to be part of it. Getting clear on this mission and vision will allow you to attract people that want to stay to be part of the solution. "If you speak something enough times with enough confidence, it then will become truth." This was a quote I heard a while back, and it stuck with me. When you talk about this mission and vision with enough confidence enough times, people will adopt it as truth and actually believe you are going to do it. They want to be part of that. There are many great companies that embody this, like ClickFunnels, Apple, and Toms.

The second part of a 3D Business is having a product or service that solves that need or problem in the world. You know that vision you just created? Now the product is literally the thing that solves that problem; rather than hoping someone else does it, solve it and be profitable while you do it. The best products in the world are the ones solving the world's biggest problems. With BDB, we went from having a product that was good by itself and trying to find people to buy it to then building a community around the mission and vision we had, my story, and the stories of other men transforming, and instead of trying to sell them our stuff, we listened to the community and created what we have today and continue to do so. This book is an example of that. You have the power to solve other people's problems and become the answer to their prayers.

The last part of a Three Dimensional Business is one of the most important and overlooked topics. Though the two things I discussed above will make you wildly profitable and sustainable, there is still something missing that could change everything for you, your clients, and the longevity and growth of your business.

The third dimension is your way to GIVE back. The world teaches us that giving makes you lose, when actually the best way to get is to give. We live in a world that tests us with games of opposites. Kind of like golf—if you want to hit the ball right, you have to swing left; if you want to hit it high, you have to hit down. It's a game of opposites. So, the most powerful way to give back through your business model is to actually give back in a way that solves the root problem of why you are in business—yes, literally having a goal to put yourself out of business. We have partnered with the Winning Edge to empower youth across America to break free from their environments and learn success principles. The youth are the future, and if we can help them become successful, discover their purpose and live a life worth modeling, then we are paying it forward. The way we do that is we build it into our business model where when a man invests in himself, we take a portion of that and invest in the cause. This allows us to always know our numbers and makes it less emotional when it comes to giving. For years I struggled with giving to causes because I felt like my money wasn't really doing anything. I was giving a little bit here and little bit there and thought it was adding up to a lot; it wasn't a lot for those causes. That's where I really dove deep into how I could partner with someone who is already putting in massive work in the area that is also connected to our core message and business so we could be more motivated to make an extreme impact. A major influence of this concept was from my mentor Cole Hatter that created an environment teaching businesses how to be profitable and make an impact at the same time—not non-profit, not for profit, but for purpose. "Thrive. Make money. Matter." By combining these three dimensions, you are setting your business up to be bulletproof all around, using the laws of success in your favor.

It hits your internal motivators, your client's internal motivators, the world's internal motivators, and your team members are even more motivated. Microsoft wanted to put a computer in every home. With that in mind, is your product or service solving the need or the problem? If not, how can it be aligned? And lastly because three strands are not easily broken, where can you give back and make it part of your business model? If you are successful, the amount you're giving raises. Look at businesses that have cracked the code on longevity and have been big players for a long time; look at how they seemingly accidentally put these core concepts together to see massive success, while others miss it completely. Remember, if you speak something enough times with enough confidence, it will soon become truth.

# Chapter 10 Action Items:

1. Are you three dimensional in the way you do business?

   _____

   _____

2. Write out what that mission and vision you have and the problem you want to solve

   _____

   _____

3. How can you incorporate giving into your business model in a way that makes sense?

   _____

   _____

4. What is your why that will keep you going when its hard?

   _____

   _____

11

# CREATE A POWER-COUPLE RELATIONSHIP

Some of the most successful people in the world give credit to their significant others. Amanda and I recently spoke at Funnel Hacking Live together because Russell loves the dynamic we have as a couple. We've been married for seven years, and I credit our success to my wife. Even if you're not in a relationship right now, this chapter is for you because one day you will be. Walt Disney, Russell Brunson, Cole Hatter, and many others say they wouldn't be where they are in life without their significant other. Yet so many people live blinded from this truth because marriage has gotten a bad rap. Society tells men that getting married means settling down, stress, having no fun, and we are losing out. But when you marry the right person who has the same vision and values as you, you are actually more powerful. Napoleon Hill says it the best in my opinion: "The number one mastermind is between husband and wife." It's a very powerful force when two people are supporting each other every single day.

### *"The number one mastermind is between husband and wife."*

Growing up, I had a lot of passions, yet I didn't have responsibilities. This clogged my brain for a long time, tricking me into thinking that I was not committed because I would pick up a hobby, and then once I got good at it, I would usually get bored and then move onto the next thing. Sadly, I would have fallen into the category of a "jack of all trades, but a master of none." I got good at bicycle racing, then moved into motocross where I gave the majority of my energy. On the side, I picked up skateboarding where I would practice hours a day if I was not riding. At a very young age, I got a set of golf clubs and would hit $20 worth of balls every day, walking with my clubs all the way to the driving range alone. I had over 300 days played on one video game, countless hours learning the guitar, studied God's spiritual principles for years upon years, became a top barista doing latte art, and kept going from hobby to hobby.

It seemed like a never-ending cycle that I would get excited about something, get good, then move on, over and over again. If it wasn't for my relationship, I would have never become the man that I am today. There is something uniquely special about a power-couple dynamic in marriage. That person who knows you better than anyone else in the world. Everyone else outside of that relationship sees you from a lens that is based on their perception and assumption, watching you and putting the pieces together. Yet there is nobody else close enough to see how you are when you sleep, how you are when you wake up, what you struggle with and what you are great at. There is nobody who knows you better, and when that person comes into alignment with who you are, they can call out a form of greatness that could have never been discovered.

I've become known over the years from my connections with a limitless amount of people with particular skills, yet a few years ago, I hated meeting new people, especially if I had to approach someone important. It was my wife who consistently saw greatness in me, who pushed me outside of my comfort zone, who didn't just call me out but called me up. This constant accountability is not pointing out what people are doing right, then telling them to do it differently; it's about keeping them in account of their ability to do something. Meaning that you see something in them that they cannot see yet, and you are calling them into that person. Now imagine how unique this is when there is someone that is not in that perception. This person knows all of your struggles and strengths, and when they actually push you and believe in you, there is no purer feeling of trust and gratefulness because it's not coming from a place of being fake. When Amanda gives me an amazing compliment, I know she is really telling the truth, and it means more to me than a complete stranger.

Anyone in the world can get a girl for a night, but can you keep her for 80 years and be in love? That's the thing we should be impressed by. I had the blessing of meeting Amanda when I was 19 years old, so we literally grew up together. So how did I attract this amazing woman? Men ask me all the time how to meet somehow like Amanda, and it's pretty simple. I don't believe in being anything different than your best self when meeting a girl. Anyone who teaches you to be someone you are not is about to put you through living hell. Whatever you do to attract someone is what you are going to have to do to keep them. Meaning that if you decide to be a complete extrovert for the night because that's what "she likes" and throw fat tips even though you are a stingy, you may be able to "pull a chick," but five years later, when the bills are due and you both are alone, lying next to each other, nobody is going to remember that moment. The purest form of attracting the right woman is by being yourself and embodying the characteristics that woman would want. Imagine yourself as bait. If you change the bait, you will change the fish. If you are the correct bait, you will attract the right fish. You should always be showing up as your best self. If you want your future wife to value herself, be willing to grow, be nice, be giving, and be attractive, then you must be that man. I attracted Amanda because we both embodied our values and were open to God's will.

Just as in business, one of the worst things people can go through is "grass is greener on the other side." That is not true. The grass is greener where you water it. If you are married right now, and she isn't giving you the love and encouragement you want, don't think of ways to leave the relationship. Think of ways to improve it, to give her the things you wished she did for you and things you know that make her happy. Take ownership of the marriage and do everything you can. You will be amazed at how it will change for the better because at one point you two were completely in love; get back to that feeling.

The majority of conventional relationships have a progression where the couple is happy for the first 10 years of the relationship, then it starts going downhill. What's interesting is it has been shown that in an arranged marriage, they have their troubles for the first 10 years because they had not fallen in love together. But because of the fact that they are committed to each other, their best years start after their first 10 years of marriage. I believe the reason is because many people get married thinking, *Well, if this doesn't work out, then we will just divorce.* They are already setting themselves up to fail. That is not commitment because every relationship will take work, and if you give up at the first sign of hardship, then you're weak. You are not a man of your word. This is not to scare you if you aren't married; this is to ensure that you understand the value of commitment and making a vow to someone else.

# Our story

Amanda and I met at a youth Christian conference on New Year's Eve 2010 in Kansas City. I flew in from San Diego with my three friends, and she drove there from Columbus with her three friends. Not knowing it at the time, I sat behind her and decided to take a picture of the conference. This picture got the back of head in it. A few months later, we both got accepted in Bethel School of Ministry and into a private Facebook Group. She posted a picture of a Ferrari jet. That picture Amanda posted automatically grabbed my attention and made me reach out. That led into more conversations and then building a relationship. What was crazy is she looked at my Facebook profile and saw the picture of the back of her head. God was trying to tell us something with this situation, and we weren't looking for a relationship at all. That Ferrari jet told me something about her, and I wanted to know more. Throughout the next few months, we developed a great friendship over the phone. It wasn't until I went to Amanda's high school graduation that we started dating. For me, having a wife that was into God and dreamed big was a value that I had. But you won't find that type of woman everywhere. You need to put yourself in an environment that she would be in and associated with. She won't be found at the strip club.

A solid foundation for any relationship is one of trust and commitment, along with realizing what each other wants out of life. Amanda and I took a pre-marriage course where everyone was engaged. At the end of the course, 50% of the couples broke up, 30% waited to get married and 20% went on to get married. For the majority of couples, the reality of life hitting them in the face and answering the questions of what they wanted in life was so real that they realized how different they were. Initial feelings and attraction can cloud your mind, so asking the hard questions is very important. The sooner those realizations can happen, the sooner everyone can move on.

> *"A solid foundation for any relationship is one of trust and commitment, along with realizing what each other wants out of life."*

Yet how do we build a proper bond in a relationship that is full of trust and intimacy? The pendulum of commitment and intimacy. The highest form of commitment in a relationship would be marriage—"Till death do us part, in sickness and in health, richer or poorer"—a pure vow of foreverness. There is nothing bigger you could really even say than those words. What's the highest level of intimacy? Sex. The bonding of two spirits together where it creates a tie between the two that is hard to undo. The lowest level of commitment with the highest form of intimacy would be like a one-night stand. As you can see, those hardly work out, and it creates a massive distrust between partners. Why? Because the gap between commitment and intimacy is all distrust. If that gap is not closed, then it's a relationship built on a foundation of distrust instead of trust. So many people wonder why their relationships are sucking, yet they jump straight into hormonal intimacy without truly getting to know somebody. By the time that phase runs off, it's too late.

They are too deep and too connected that they just live in a sub-par relationship until it all comes crashing down.

When Amanda and I first started talking, we got lucky that it was virtually because we lived in two different states, so we had to get to know each other without any intimacy at first. I never kissed her until we started dating and I felt that it was right because I didn't want to create distrust. We then continued this all the way through until marriage where we didn't have sex until we were married. Many women are giving a man all the goods and benefits without any of the commitment. Why would he put more skin in the game in the relationship if there is no reward? When intimacy is higher than commitment, there is no reason for us to feel like committing, yet to respect a woman, the best way is by doing it this way.

Inside of a relationship, it has been shown that either a man or a woman can lead. It's completely wrong, just not in the way most people would think. Of course, women can lead, and a lot of times they can better than a man. Yet it is still the man's job to be the leader in the relationship when it comes to vision and burden. I would never ever tell my wife to go outside and check who is breaking into the house because she is the "leader." Nor send her out to war before me. Why? Because I am the man of the freaking house, and that's my role, and it always will be. A king and a queen run a castle, a kingdom, together. Every king needs a queen. The queen is not lesser than the king but can actually operate in the same level of authority and increasing authority as the king's authority increases. Yet she takes on zero percent of the burden, allowing her to be extremely powerful because the consequence of failure and problems fall on the king. It's truly powerful to women for men to lead because it empowers them to be able to reach a potential they could not ever reach. When women don't have to carry the burden of everything, they then can go after their dreams and operate in a more feminine energy. You as the man are the leader of your relationship. Do you feel that way? Are you acting that way? Would she say you are? These are great questions to ask yourself.

> *"Inside of a relationship, there are many different personality types at play, roles, and love languages."*

Inside of a relationship, there are many different personality types at play, roles, and love languages. These can be extremely helpful tools to help navigate and understand relationships and yourself better. By understanding your personality type, it can help with knowing your strengths and weaknesses along with your partner's. Myers Briggs and the DISC are two personalities tests that I recommend. It will make you understand and celebrate your differences. I also highly recommend Gary Chapman's book *The Five Love Languages* if you haven't read it already. Amanda's primary love language is physical touch, and mine is quality time. This was a huge learning curve when we get together because I never showed PDA, and so she thought I didn't like her physically. Now that we know these things, we use these tools to make our relationship stronger. The five love languages are physical touch, quality time, acts of service, gifts, and words of affirmation. If you haven't taken the test yet, you can go on the website or buy the book.

Understanding roles is super important. It's even more important for a married couple than those just dating because there is a greater commitment when it comes to a home, finances, chores, and so many other things. One of the best ways to find out those roles is to connect together every day, go over what you are grateful for, what is on your to-do list for that day, what your intention is for the day, and to express the areas that you are feeling uncomfortable. This allows for good, productive conversation about things that most people would just brush under the rug. In these talks, you can also establish responsibilities, boundaries, and expectations. This is not always going to work, and it won't eliminate problems entirely. You would be a damn robot if it did. See when you have commitment, problems = love. Here is why love grows as you get to know and discover someone you love more. When you have conflict, the only thing that gets you through it is commitment to the relationship, or else we would all walk away. Now the commitment gets you to have the conversation that would not be worth having with someone you weren't committed to. On the other side of the conversation is a greater understanding of each other. On the other side of that is a greater level of love that has never been experienced before.

Most people get stuck in the mud, never getting to the promised land on the other side of commitment getting you through conflict. Three-dimensional relationships are the most important aspect of a 3D Businessman's life because he doesn't just have the same nine-to-five clocking in and clocking out. There are seasons, things change, problems arise, and things are constantly changing and moving where priorities get tested every single day. When Amanda and I first got married, we were completely broke, not knowing what to do. I was trying to dig holes and do whatever I could to make some money. Being a businessman, we went through so many different seasons that most relationships would never make it through because they are not exercising the power-couple dynamic. From broke, to schedule changes, to small apartments, to carpet cleaning, to selling things at 10:00 p.m. on Craigslist—the list goes on and on. I remember when we first started planning for our first live event. Prior to the promotion, we would come home, my wife and I would eat dinner, we would work out every day together and enjoy ourselves at night. Then, all the sudden, the event promotion came. I had less time in the gym and less time to watch a show or hang out.

If that was not communicated in any way, our relationship would have been on the rocks, like most relationships are. When there is expectation without communication, it creates cancer in the relationship. I want to share with you the three core ingredients that have helped Amanda and I grow deeper in love together and work as a team.

# Unified Vision

This isn't something that someone does one time; it's consistent, day to day. When I was promoting the live event, we both understood what needed to be done, why it needed to be done, and how it was going to be done. When I was working long hours and missing normal activities, it didn't take Amanda by surprise because she understood the what and why and was in alignment. We knew that these events were a step to give us the life that we wanted. So many relationships don't have an aligned vision. I remember one of my clients, who is the top dog trainer in San Diego. One time he was in my office with his assistant and wife, and they were talking about how the board and trains (where the dogs live with them for a certain amount of time) were the most stressful things in the business and their relationship. Yet they always wanted to open up their own place, which would solve the entire problem. They never got there because they never took on enough board and trains to get to that point because it was too hard. We broke down what they wanted. They wanted more freedom and more income in their business and life. We broke down why they wanted it. We broke down how they were going to get it and the how was doing the very thing they hated. However, it became something they didn't hate because they knew it was for a purpose. They were aligned in the goal. They were able to go all in together for a short amount of time to get to the life that they wanted. It takes a unified vision to get out of the desert into the promised land. Long term and short term.

Many of the men I work with come to me saying, "My wife doesn't have the same goals as me. What's wrong with her?" It's okay to have different goals, but you two must come together on a big vision. The way to get her to support your goals is to first ask and listen to her goals. Keep digging until you see what lights her up, and then support her in those. She might not always get why you want to work out five times a week, but if you are trying to pursue a speaking career and she hates it, then you need to communicate the importance and why behind it.

# Commitment

I have touched on this subject a lot in this book, so I think you get the point. A three-dimensional relationship takes a full-on commitment to yourself and to your partner. Relationships unravel where doubt meets distraction. Be a man who is trustworthy because of his actions, not just his words.

# Over-Communication

This is something that we have always done in our relationship to a fault we believed. We do not let the sun go down on a problem. We solve the problem or build understanding around it before we move onto other things. This has been a core foundation of our relationship because we have our relationship as a higher priority than our business or anything else besides ourselves. Many can talk the talk, but they can't walk the walk. It takes strong, consistent communication to live as a power couple and break into new atmospheres every single day—not allowing things to get swept under the rug; not allowing things to be miscommunicated or misinterpreted.

> *"When a relationship is starting, it's all about coming together as two people who have genuine interest in who each other are."*

When a relationship is starting, it's all about coming together as two people who have genuine interest in who each other are. Communicating a vision and coming into agreement with that vision will make you unstoppable. Once the commitment is made, maximize it by applying the power-couple dynamic, which is like steroids to the relationship. Continual unified vision is needed because being a businessman isn't like being married to an employee. Communicate every single day and carve out that time where it's just the two of you. If it's a priority, you will make time for it. This is a 3D relationship; this is the power couple dynamic.

Amanda and I have been building businesses together since the day we got married. We didn't have a choice. We were broke, and two seemed better than one in getting that problem solved. Throughout the years, we discovered massive truths to operate at an Olympic level together while maximizing our relationship first. Always keep the relationship fun and growing above all things. Have a lot of sex and deeply understand each other's desires and goals. You and your wife should not be the same, and if you are, you will see one day that you are not. Celebrate those differences.

These concepts I share in this chapter might be unfamiliar because hundreds of years ago, we were taught this by our fathers. Yet at some point, our fathers started going off to work rather than being at home more. We stayed home with our mom and learned how to be a man based on what a woman would want. Then we go to school where the majority of teachers are female. Then, somehow at 18, we are supposed to know how to be a man with never being shown what a man truly is. We've grown up thinking that if we just are a good person and do the right things, we will be happy and have all of our needs met. My friend Dr. Robert Glover wrote a book, *No More Mr. Nice Guy*, which breaks this down in further detail. This couldn't be further from the truth. Take 100 percent responsibility for yourself and your relationships today. Nice guys finish last; leaders finish first, meaning that nice guys make sure everyone else gets what they want instead of taking care of themselves first. Women are looking for leaders who have value for themselves. Ever notice that most women are attracted to the bad dude? That's because those men are confident in who they are and their decisions. They aren't looking for a woman to lead them; they are the leader.

Your intimate relationship will be the most empowering or disempowering thing in your life. Choose your partner wisely. Show up as the leader she wants. Put her above your business. Put her above your children. Make her feel valued by how much you know her and care. Most of the time, women just want to be heard. They don't want you to solve their problems. You have two ears and one mouth for a reason. Many people think that a marriage is 50/50, but it's not. It's 100/100. Invest in your marriage above all else because your happiness, your success, and your legacy are counting on it.

# Chapter 11 Action Items:

1.  Write down everything you want in a woman, even if you are married. How can you embody the attributes and characteristics that would attract someone like that?

    _____

    _____

2.  Set aside a time to get clear on your vision for the relationship and what you want to accomplish. Make sure you ask her for her opinion and incorporate her goals.

    _____

    _____

3.  Are you letting other things come before your wife? If so, how can you make sure she knows she is more valuable than those other things.

    _____

    _____

4.  Would you say that your love languages are filled up? If not, communicate that and invest more time into fulfilling her love languages.

    _____

    _____

12

# CREATING A LEGACY

D o you remember the story at the end of Chapter 1 about the
guy who rushed my truck in the middle of the night and had
tattoos covering his whole body? I wanted to make sure I rewarded
you by making it to the last chapter of this book to finish it. The end
of this story may have shaped my life a lot more than I would have
thought at the time.

I wanted to be used by God, as I still do, and I remember like
yesterday when he rushed my truck. I had no clue what to do to
stop him, so I blurted out the first thing I thought of, and he stopped
in his tracks. He looked extremely confused, as he stared at me, and
me back at him. He asked me, "What the heck are you doing here,
and why would you say that?"

At this point I was just happy to still be alive, yet I had no clue where to go from there. I asked him, "Where are you going?"

He said, "To my house." So, of course, I asked if I could give him a ride, and he said yes. So now here I am in the middle of nowhere in the middle of the night with a guy in my truck, who is twice my size with tattoos from his feet to his neck, who had just rushed my truck minutes earlier. Not only that; this guy was talking to himself in my passenger seat!

He continued to have a troubled look on his face, wondering why the heck I stopped for him. I let him know that I felt I was being used by God to do something big, but obviously tonight it might have just been to drive someone home. Yet at that moment he started freaking out and crying. I had no clue if he was just crying in general or if I made him cry and it would then turn into rage again. So I asked him, "Is everything alright?"

He replied, "My car broke down, and I was on the hill, and I was thinking if I should go home or not, and I didn't know what to do, and all these things keep piling up on me, and terrible things keep happening one after another..."

I thought to myself, *Where the heck is he going with all this?*

He continued, "My car broke down, and that was the last straw for me. I walked up on the hill and looked down at my car, which was like a representation of my life. On the outside it looked like a car, but really it was broke and couldn't move. I felt worthless. So, I decided in that moment that it was finally time to take my own life, to kill myself. Yet I had nothing to kill myself with, so I decided to walk home and kill myself at my house. So, I started walking with no shoes on back to my place when you drove past me in your truck. Not one person drove by when I was on that hill, but all the sudden, when I was walking you drove by, and I saw you turn into that parking lot, and the only thing that went through my mind was, *If that person stops I'm going to beat the shit out of him.* And when you came around the corner, that's what I was going to do." And he started crying like a child in the passenger seat of my truck as I was driving him home.

We arrived at his house, prayed together, and this was the moment that changed everything for him. A man who had no hope, who was literally walking to his death, got interrupted by some random 18-year-old kid who was willing to be led, who was willing to listen to that voice inside of him and do something bigger than himself. And right away I got to experience the power of my friend taking her own life. Though I could never bring her back, I could make her life mean something. Right away, I got to see the fruit of that from seeing this man's life changed. You don't have to change the world by reaching a lot of people; it all starts with stopping for the person in front of you and making an impact in their life. This man and I are still friends on Facebook to this day, and he now has a family.

## Leave It All on the Field

The number one thing people die with is regrets. They look back not at what they did and did wrong but the things they didn't do. I ask people, "If there was a movie made about your whole life, would you actually want to watch it?"

Want to know how you leave life feeling like you left it all on the field?

As businessmen, we are always looking at how we can win, how we can check goals off the list, how we can push ourselves to be more and do more. How can we always be progressing in every moment? If we are not going forward, we are going backwards. My friend once told me a story about him and his grandpa. This friend of mine was going after his career at full speed and was making tons of money, working with the second biggest company, which allowed him to travel the world. He was so excited about his progress. One day he had a conversation with his grandfather, who was impressed by what he was doing, and a clear moment of wisdom came. His grandfather said, "Wow, it really looks like you are climbing the corporate ladder."

My friend replied, "Yeah, I really am."

His grandpa said back to him, "How do you know your ladder is against the right wall?"

This shook my friend and made him question why he was doing it. He ended up leaving his position, which had a clear path to riches, success, and achievement because he knew in that moment he wasn't doing what he felt was right. One of my coaches coached with Tony Robbins for over a decade, and one of the hardest things to teach was good intuition, the ability the be fulfilled and follow an internal guidance; yet if people could get that one thing, everything else would follow.

I fell into the benefit of the spiritual law when I was 18 years old; "I would rather do what I know is right and fail then do what is wrong and succeed." So how does this relate to every man? Well, the world will give you a version of success that by definition is the world's. We can go our entire life doing what we know is wrong, and succeeding in everyone else's eyes, gaining our validation by the fact that we are "doing the right thing," "the logical safe thing," only to arrive at the grave with one of the most poisonous realities: regret. Remember, as mentioned earlier, without vision, a man will die, physically or even worse, internally. If there is anything I could give you from this book, it wouldn't just be the blueprints, the skeletons, the action items of what to follow to see success but the actual ability for you to see and achieve what you are born to do. The ability to feel/see a leading and actually follow it. To feel the sense of flow when you are living, not just the life that everyone else says you should live, but your life. Just because something is good, doesn't mean it's right. I was talking to my Navy Seal mentor a few years ago about designing the life that I wanted. I was telling him that I basically wanted to be Tony Stark—same house, same stuff, everything. He laughed and brought an overwhelming correction as well that didn't feel good for quite a few days. He said, "That's great, and that's what everyone else would have you do, but at some point, you are going to have to figure out what life YOU actually want." How did I know he was right? Because I felt that punch in my stomach knowing that what I was saying wasn't 100 percent true. See, it's okay to take other people's dreams that you look up to, model their goals, and be inspired. Similar to writing music, you first figure out how to play other people's music before you learn how to play your own. Yet so many of us tend to continue following other people's versions of success, which leads us to know our own version of failure.

## "Just because something is good, doesn't mean it's right."

You are a unique businessman. You have the only fingerprint that is like yours. You have a unique place in the world and a destiny that looks nothing like anybody else's. So, what is the life that you want to create? What are things you want to do? What is impact you want to make? What are the things you want to accomplish? What are your core values as a man? The richest place in the world is the graveyard. It's where the best ideas, creativity, talent, potential, and destiny goes unfulfilled. We can spend our lives checking things off a checklist over and over again to wind up at a destination that we never planned. You can take steps every day, but what destination are you looking to arrive at? The starting point of success begins at the end, not the beginning. The goal of life is not to get to the end without a scratch, arriving safely at the grave without ever doing anything wrong.

Inside of our highest-level programs, we jump into these aspects regularly with the perspective that you are alive for a reason, and you still have things to do on this earth or you wouldn't be here. Imagine the lives of people that were taken early and how badly they would want a second chance to come back and do things correctly. With this newfound understanding, imagine them watching the lives of men alive today. If for all of eternity every living thing had to watch your life on repeat, would it be worth watching? Would you feel comfortable and confident with what you did here? See, if I were to watch a movie for eternity, I would rather watch the man who gave it his all, leaving nothing on the field, than the guy who succeeded using 30 percent of his potential.

Take a minute to actually picture everyone in the world, alive and dead, having to watch your life for all of eternity. What different decisions would you be making now? For the fathers out there or future fathers, what is the legacy you are looking to create for your family? What is the meaning you want to bring to your family name? Many of us have family names that really have no meaning in this earth. Do you want to change that? What's the example you would want to leave for your family and kids? Imagine that every decision that you make in life, you are passing down to your kid so that when the time comes, they will make that same decision. As a businessman, you are creating your personal brand every single day through influence. You have influence over people whether you know it or not, and whether you like it or not, it's your moral obligation to take responsibility for that influence.

# Unleashing Your Power

How would you like to tap into greater confidence?

One of the hardest things in a man's life is when the information in his head and his dreams are bigger than his results. One of the characteristics of a successful businessman is being able to make decisions today based on where he is going, not where he is right now.

This was one of the hardest things I went through when I was carpet cleaning every day, then trying to show up to networking events, closing deals—shoot, just talking to anyone. I looked at myself as the carpet cleaner and I thought everyone could see right through me and see that. Then, one day, I was sitting on the floor of my mother and father in law's house and I lay down, listened to music, and started dreaming. I knew that what got me here would not get me there; that somehow the most powerful men in the world knew the beginning from the end and made decisions based on where they are going not where they are at.

I knew the only way I would ever live the life I wanted was if instead of waiting for the world around me to transform me and grow me, I had to take the world inside of me and have it shift the world around me. I knew the life I wanted was in my head, but it didn't look that way on the outside. So, I laid there and dreamed up what life would be like in a year if I did what I wanted to do. Five years, 10 years, 20 years down the road, who would I be? And though I couldn't think of the "things" that I would have because I didn't know if I'd be flying spaceships or what the heck I'd be doing, I did see the man I was going to become. If everything went well, what man would you become? What type of confidence would you have and feel 20 years from now? What will you have accomplished? How do you live your life and spend time? How confident are you in your decision-making abilities? I literally sat there and started listing off all the qualities of my future self in detail. It felt so good; I was so pumped to become that one day. Then it hit me. I wasn't supposed to just learn from my future self; I am actually called to be my future self now, and then allow the world to shift around me until I create that reality.

Most men go through life playing life's rules, hoping just their environment transforms them. I do the opposite; I choose to change the environment. I made a decision in that moment that I would be myself 20 years from now and physically switch places with that person. I'm not faking who I am but actually becoming something now that I will be because I can finally see the beginning from the end. So, imagine the life you want to create, and don't just mentally masturbate and dream up of all the cool things that "could" happen in your life but actually have an experience and encounter with your future self and emotionally connect with who you are becoming. Then decide to trade places with that guy and remind yourself of that reality every day.

### *"Most men go through life playing life's rules, hoping just their environment transforms them."*

When I am writing, speaking in front of thousands, coaching, and teaching, whatever it is, I constantly remind myself of this concept because without it, I wouldn't even be able to put these words to paper. I wouldn't be able to serve the people we are serving. It was in that moment that I made that decision, and it was in that moment that my confidence changed. I wasn't operating as a carpet cleaner. I was the successful version of myself having an experience as a carpet cleaner. If you went back in time 10 years with what you know now, would you be more successful? The answer is always yes; this is the power this creates. Invest your time to dream up what your dream life looks like; it will always be evolving. Keep listening to that internal voice guiding you and become the man you want to become today; shift the world around you until they see that reality. Allow the truths in this book to be your North Star, your playbook to forever winning as not just a businessman but a Modern Day Businessman creating success without sacrifice.

So many men get caught up in only the result they are producing and not the process they are going through to produce that result. If you were to go back in time one year and see how you have grown, or even if you were able to go back a year knowing what you know now, would you be more successful? The answer is yes, so then try 5 years, 10 years, 20 years ago (if you can); if you can go back that far in time, would life have been easier? How much have you grown as a person in your confidence, understanding, knowledge, etc.? The same way hindsight is 20/20 is the exact same thing you will experience doing this from the future to the present. Like I said before, the majority of the people at their grave look back at the things that they didn't do and regret. Live a life with no regrets; live a life we would want to watch; live a life that has meaning. You as a man carry your last name that is passed down to your children and your children's children. This is your opportunity to bring honor to your family name, to create a legacy for your family that is passed down and rewarded for generations. You, as the man, the Modern Day Businessman, hold these keys. If you hold the principles in this book close to your heart, anything is possible. The world is looking for a man who rises up and says, "pick me," then shows up every day to do the work. There is no competition in this area because most men live life with bumper lanes on, trying not to make a mistake to arrive at the finish line with no scratches, never fully living.

Use that intuition, the calling, the guide that you have on your life and take action on that still small voice continually to create the life that you want. The first step is committing 100 percent to success. One of my favorites is of Alexander the Great. Alexander was one of the greatest officers of war of all time, never losing a battle. During these wars, they didn't have radio or communication yet, so the way they would communicate during war would be to have a drummer play a tune that meant something like "retreat" or "attack," and then the next one would play it, and so on. One time, Alexander was under huge attack at his home and had realized that there was no way that they were going to be able to defend themselves. So, he had turned to the drummer that was next to him that had been serving with him for several years and yelled at him, "PLAY RETREAT."

The drummer then looked at him with a stunned look on his face.

After a few seconds, Alexander yelled at him again, "PLAY RETREAT!"

The drummer still stood there trembling. Was he in shock? Was he confused? No, this man looked at Alexander the Great and told him, "I never learned how to play retreat."

"WHAT?! You don't know how to play retreat. How is that possible? You have been playing alongside me for years!"

The man looked at him and said, "I never thought we would need to play it. We have never played it before." So, because he had no clue how to play retreat, instead they played "attack." They went on to win that battle only because retreating was not an option. See, when you have no choice but to push forward, miracles happen. Take "retreat" out of your vocabulary.

*"When you have no choice but to push forward, miracles happen."*

# Chapter 12 Action Items:

1. Where do you want to be in five years? What does life look like?

   _____

   _____

2. Reflect back on how much you have grown over the last five years. What are the key things you are proud of yourself for?

   _____

   _____

3. Write down three things that you currently want to do more of that make you happy?

   _____

   _____

4. What do you want people to remember you by?

_____

_____

5. Picture who you are going to be 10 to 20 years from now and embody the confidence that man has.

_____

_____

*Thank you and congratulations for completing this journey of The Modern Day Businessman! I hope this inspires you to make your mess your message and you have come to believe that you can have success without sacrifice. I look forward to seeing you in The Billion Dollar Brotherhood so we can support you in becoming a Three-Dimensional Businessman and help you create a new family legacy. If this book impacted you, I would be honored to hear about it. I will personally reply back to any message on Facebook, Instagram, a review on Amazon, or an e-mail to my team.*

# JOIN THE BILLION DOLLAR BROTHERHOOD FACEBOOK GROUP

Connect with Nicholas and thousands of other like minded businessmen.

# GRAB EXCLUSIVE TRAININGS FROM ME HERE WWW. NICHOLASBAYERLE. COM/ OFFERS